SELECTED POEMS

A CENTENNIAL BOOK

One hundred books
published between 1990 and 1995
bear this special imprint of
the University of California Press.
We have chosen each Centennial Book
as an example of the Press's finest
publishing and bookmaking traditions
as we celebrate the beginning of
our second century.

UNIVERSITY OF CALIFORNIA PRESS

Founded in 1893

SELECTED POEMS
CHARLES OLSON

EDITED BY ROBERT CREELEY

UNIVERSITY OF CALIFORNIA PRESS

BERKELEY
LOS ANGELES
OXFORD

University of California Press
Berkeley and Los Angeles, California

University of California Press, Ltd.
Oxford, England

Library of Congress Cataloging-in-Publication Data
Olson, Charles, 1910–1970.
    Selected poems / Charles Olson ; edited by Robert Creeley.
      p.   cm.
    "A Centennial book."
    Includes index.
    ISBN 0-520-07528-5
    I. Creeley, Robert, 1926–   . II. Title.
   PS3529.L655A6   1993
   811'.54—dc20   92-23838

Printed in the United States of America
9 8 7 6 5 4 3 2 1

The publisher gratefully acknowledges the contribution provided by the General Endowment
Fund of the Associates of the University of California Press.

The paper used in this publication meets the minimum requirements of the American National
Standard for Information Sciences—Permanence of Paper for Printed Library Materials, ANSI
Z39.48-1984. ∞

CONTENTS

II [from *THE MAXIMUS POEMS*]

PREFACE

A characteristic of our time has been its insistent preoccupation with system. Possibly other periods have been so engaged, but, for the fast fading twentieth century, that order which may govern all data, theoretical or substantive, proves a question affecting far more than simple authority. One recognizes that such a call to order has many guises and applications, whether these be political, philosophic, scientific, or poetic. A system, which can significantly accommodate the apparent world, must recognize the plurality and the density of that world, the increasing factors of persons if also the shrinking of their physical provision. It must admit their variousness, while accommodating their equally stable needs. It must deal with what is as it might be, yet never lose hold of the given.

It is tempting to see the first defining poets of our century as heroic, almost necessarily so. Ezra Pound's epic attempt to make a long poem "including history," to give us the requisite "tales of the tribe," so that a measure for human values might be secured, is profoundly moving. If, finally, he cannot, in his own words, "make it cohere," he has nonetheless entered the apparent chaos of existence as a surviving witness, though his "errors and wrecks" lie about him. The system which was to institute a lasting order, the fascism in which he sadly trusted, failed him, leaving only his art.

So too seem T. S. Eliot's determinations, the conviction that an order is carried by tradition from a past wherein all values are defined. Therefore his system is adamantly conservative. As he recognizes the society's impending loss of faith and definition, he holds fast to the securing tenets of established pattern. But, with time, his proposal seems an increasingly wistful predication, at best consummately artful, at worst a didactic and isolating habit.

But it is not only the compulsive rush of "things" or the chaotic impact of all those other disjunctive "worlds" that must be made manageable. Clearly the loss of articulate response resulting from an overwhelming dogmatism or the chaos which comes of indulged confusions is both familiar and destructive. But a simplifying reduction of any of these factors merely must prove a useless giving over of all that variousness on which our humanity must finally depend. A system must recognize, as William Carlos Williams insisted, "Only the imagination is real," which fact proves both its limit and our possibility. Many applications of human potential have only to do with static ends in view, or products, call them, of previous desire and decision. One will hardly regret that an active agriculture can feed us, but the endless provisions for thus predetermined wars cannot be so simply agreed to. There are imaginations that differ absolutely in their use of legitimizing purpose, yet each defines a potential.

Much that has been questioned as difficult in poetry has to do with just such matters. A poetry which has as its function the maintenance of a securely familiar pattern will not easily admit an alternative which seeks to locate order in the "phenomenal world which is raging and yet apart," as D. H. Lawrence had written in *The Escaped Cock*, a work that Olson very much respected. There Jesus says to Mary Magdalene, "The day of my interference is done . . . ," and, a little later, "The recoil fails the advance." Such "objectism," in Charles Olson's terms, defeated a simplifying humanism that read "human" as the apex of ordering condition and all else as along for the ride. The same sense is found also in another of Olson's crucial sources, Alfred North Whitehead, in the qualification of human as "ego object in field of objects." The emphasis is insistent.

It has been easy enough to read Olson as simply the continuity from Pound and Williams, who each attempted, with the *Cantos* and *Paterson* respectively, to find a defining measure for our common lives. Yet these two poets are themselves significantly at odds, and what each presumes as the potential and necessity of their undertaking argues for a necessary recognition that "a new world is only a new mind, and the poem and the mind are all apiece." The very trust that Williams, in such a phrase, accorded the imagination may find much parallel in Pound, but Pound's late comment that he regretted not having had Williams' humanity might find complement in Williams' lifelong dilemma with his social fact as a poet.

What Olson seemingly insists upon is the scale possible, the size one is capable of, the field, as he puts it, of one's energies and engagements. He says, "Come into the world" and "Take a big bite," admonishing those who "can take no risk that matters, the risk of beauty least of all." He proposes that *space* is the "first fact" of our present existence, and that we "are the last first people," an echo still resonant of the locating movement of human life to constitute place, or, for Olson, "having descried the nation / to write a Republic / in gloom on Watch-House Point."

In general, such proposals, which have a diverse yet recurrent presence in his work, may seem all too familiar to the American reader, battered with "New Frontiers" and the inevitably shrunken prospect of an "outer space" that might, one hoped, accommodate the pinched and habituated appetite of that inner world where all seems always insufficient. But one sees quickly the difference in that Olson is not persuaded by a "change" that merely redistributes the terms of such containment without moving to recognize and determine what *are* those "limits which any of us are inside of." His question, then, is how can humans be so stated, so located, as to give their potential lives the full range of that possibility. In short, what is humanness, call it, what are its parameters, its givens, its determining histories, its collective biology, its company and investment upon the earth?

Here he may be said to separate from either Pound or Williams, and certainly from Eliot, in that all three variously depended upon a box or frame which, for Olson's determinants, was inadequate. For example, Pound's backed on the Renaissance, to which limit Eliot added a rigidly fixed classicism, while Williams, if more questioning of such measures, still could not open the locked world of his *Paterson* to that new "mind" he so longed to see realized. The "blueberry America" of his imagination, as Olson called it, could not answer to the confounding realities surrounding.

The materials of Olson's poetry come from a remarkable diversity of sources, both with respect to their information and to their fact of origin. Olson's note in his defining essay, "Projective Verse," that the poet "will have some several causes" alludes simply to what becomes in his own practice an extraordinary conversion of data and modes of consciousness. For one instance, "The Librarian" is not only a paradigmatic statement of Olson's situation, literally, in Gloucester but is as well, factually, a dream. So too the crucial image of his mother in "As the Dead Prey Upon Us," and all the attendant action, are facts thus taken. What is most to be emphasized is that two such determinations of reality can so meld, work the same street, as it were, without loss of coherence or particularity, and so fuse as a complex and far more inclusive apprehension of what, after all, our human ways of knowing have as root.

Always Olson's intent was to break through any compartmentalizing of such information, that is, to demonstrate, as such poems surely do, that our information is not a mere context of "subjects" nor our ways of knowing only a reductively diurnal "rationalism." So he will enter from a wide range of "grounds," those places wherein his thought and feeling are moved to form words much as one can hear this very act occurring in the early "La Chute."

Interestingly enough, the text of this poem transforms in turn a translation, recasting fragments provided by the Sumerologist Samuel Noah Kramer to make a percussive, intensively active drama from a surviving ritual employed to secure tradition's function, so as to carry over from the dead the vivifying agency, the insistent pulse. Most exceptional, however, is his use of Arthur Rimbaud's reputed last poem, "O saisons, o châteaux," as the ground for "Variations Done for Gerald Van De Wiele," in which that work becomes a base from which he moves three interlocking readings of Rimbaud's initial text with increasing emphasis and power. To call such a poem either translation or adaptation only is to mistake how Olson uses the initiating work as material, not as a static accomplishment to be restated by presumptive report or description.

There is another accuracy which Olson far more valued, a reading competent to hear all that the source might provoke—"where the dry blood talks / where the old appetite walks," as he writes in "The Kingfishers." This was to be his first poem of characteristic scale and authority. In it he offers what are to prove givens of his circumstance, that "What does not change / is the will to change," that "the feed-back is / the law . . . ," and that "Despite the discrepancy (an ocean   courage   age)" one (as Rimbaud, as any so engaged) must undertake the "risk" of primary recognitions, of knowing in literal sense our own histories and nature, of breaking through the enclosing generalities and fictions of whatever form keeps back the initial energies of art itself. "Art is the only true twin life has."

No doubt the complex premises on which *The Maximus Poems* depend are far more various in their sources than any quick rehearsal will suggest. But at least one may note a few of their qualifications. For example, there is the obvious factor of Olson's own physical size, about 6'8", and the equally relevant sense of rhetorical stance which he worked to accomplish, an "address," as he would say, capable of encompassing the full range of human "history" in all the extensive facts of "place," the *topos* he emphasizes, with *tropos* and *typos*, as being, together, the three determinants of human condition. History was " '*istorin*," which Olson took from Herodotus and used not as a noun or concept, but, rather, as a verb, *"to find out for yourself."* Always at root is the impelling fact of working to discover, to recover, the radical *presence* of person he felt to have been lost and to regain authority for the innate coherence of whatever it is that we propose as life.

The Maximus Poems begin in form as letters, frequently political, overtly committed to social and economic measures of "polis," which for Olson constituted the full and determining company of the social body. Thus the poem's Maximus relates to the historical Maximus of Tyre, second century A.D., found by Olson while reading about Sappho. The agency inherent in the philosopher's archaic relation to the practical actions of a society, as Aristotle's to Alexander, for one instance, was attractive also.

Gloucester itself, the grounding element for all of Olson's material, was his childhood's alternative to the Worcester he otherwise lived in.

Summers, the Olsons would share with like families the various housing which permitted them all to get out of inland industrial cities as Worcester to the proverbial seashore Gloucester provided. This port on the sea side of Cape Ann north of Boston first locates the New World's fishing industry. Begun in the early seventeenth century by Rev. John White and those soon following, Gloucester is a densely layered accumulation of that early settlement and the mercantile interests underlying. So, in Olson's employment, Gloucester resonates with insistently repetitive patterns of human use and value. At points his measure is literally a foot by foot pacing, at others the whole geologic, slow shifting of a continent's strata. Time equally resounds through the surviving instance of a path, the facing of a building, the protecting boulders which front a cove. Olson was fond of John Smith's definition: "History is the memory of time." In the statement's dependence upon that human possibility, it has power both to recognize and to convert the otherwise inert facts to counters of the necessarily communal story. Like myth, it becomes "what was said of what was said."

The continuing sequence of poems, "tesserae," as Olson was to call them, moved focus and materials in a way more a compact of evidences than simply a narrative. That is, he followed the lead of his own inquiry and of what that then led to. The dimensions are therefore soon shifted from the measure of one's own story—Olson was to insist that the poem was not significantly autobiographical—or even those stories of a precedent history. Rather, one enters a contiguously related world of "eternal event," which phrase Olson derived from his reading of Whitehead, a moment which is not so much timeless as manifest in all conditions of time. So the work grows in a complex of apparent directions, both *out*, cosmologically, and *in*, to intensive issues of the nature, the minute particulars, of a "self." Again these factors intersect, in evident history, as in "Maximus, in Gloucester Sunday, LXV," where the proposed company displaces of necessity any simple "time." So too in "Celestial evening, October 1967" Olson creates such scale, that all static presumptions of reality are transformed—"and I // hear all, the new moon new in all / the ancient sky."

What changes immensely in the few years separating Williams' *Paterson* from Olson's *Maximus* is the literal configuration of that world which each attempts to salvage. All previous epistemological structures and, even more, their supporting cultural referents were displaced significantly, if not forever, by the political, economic, and technological transformations following the Second World War. The underlying causes were well in place at the turn of the century but by 1950 the effects were even more dominant. There could no longer be such a "father/son" disposition of reality as either Pound or Williams, tacitly, took as a given of their situation. Olson's displacement echoes painfully in his own undertakings, and nowhere more so than in "I have been an ability—a machine . . ."

It was Pound's proposal that "points define a periphery." So these notes serve, however inadequately, that same possibility. Were the world a determination of fixed reference and stable content, then all might be plotted with secure conviction and assurance. But if our time can claim any securing sign for its passage, it is its absolutely chaotic—*entropic*, one wants to say—malfunction in all its vital activities, whether political or economic, which prove, finally, to be the abiding rule.

But a simplifying cynicism was not a part of Olson's disposition, despite he well knew the characteristic uses of power in political office. Given his authority within the Democratic party of the last years of Roosevelt's presidency, he might well have had a very different life had he chosen to join that meager club. Instead he cast off as a poet, following the provocative success of his compactly profound study of Melville, *Call Me Ishmael*, and is otherwise identified as the rector of Black Mountain College, the prototypical "experimental college" of this country's history. From there to increasingly isolated and difficult circumstances of living was a harshly small distance.

My own part here needs qualification because of necessity I have assumed a great deal in the selection of the poems to follow from such a large and various number, making of them a context unavoidably my own despite what the poems themselves equally and with initiating purpose "have to say." Finally I could look to no advice but the long held habit of our use of one another, during his life, to act as a measure, a bearing, an unabashed response to what either might write or say. The several volumes of our letters to one another, *Charles Olson & Robert Creeley: The Complete Correspondence*, will best serve as instance. I had also the responsibility of helping to resolve several crucial texts for him, beginning with *In Cold Hell* and *Mayan Letters* in 1953. In a poem he thanked me with such generosity, saying I'd given him "the world," and then made me "the Figure of Outward" in the dedication of his *Maximus Poems*—which fact sustains me here.

George Butterick is the crucial editor of Olson's work at large: *The Maximus Poems, The Collected Poems of Charles Olson*, and the final volume of his uncollected poems, *A Nation of Nothing but Poetry*, as well as other collections of his prose and plays. It is Butterick to whom we owe the survival of all the evidence of Olson's genius as a poet. For a sense of Olson's work otherwise, I've felt always that his peers were those most capable with such help, as, for example, the notes of either Robert Duncan or Edward Dorn, or such a book as John Clarke's *From Feathers to Iron*. For a grounding information of his extraordinary life, I recommend Tom Clark's primary study, *Charles Olson: The Allegory of a Poet's Life*.

When there was first the possibility of assembling this book, I felt much intimidated by the responsibility. Yet when I read to discover just what might be the choice, it seemed to me evident almost without question. It is to the point that in the exceptional scale and range of Olson's work a place of intimate order abides. Thus "the fundament stays as put as the firmament." Each of us must find our own way. "By ear, he sd . . ."

This edition is fact of a wide range of affection and support from a generous number of people I can only begin to thank here. Among them are Charles Peter Olson, Robert Grenier, Duncan McNaughton, Al Glover, William McPheron, Richard Fyffe, Ralph Maud, Jack Clarke, Lew Daly, Charles Bernstein, Alex Katz, Barbara Ras, Barbara Jellow, Ben Friedlander, R. B. Kitaj, and Tom Clark, all of whom helped to make most specifically this present book.

The text follows George Butterick's editorial determinations in the two University of California Press publications, *The Maximus Poems* (1983) and *The Collected Poems* (1987), with exceptions on these few pages: 28, 30, 55, 96, 177, 180, 189, 199, 220. These changes were based upon my understanding of the texts in question and are solely my responsibility.

Robert Creeley

I   [from *Collected Poems*]

Move Over

Merchants.   of the sea and of finance

(Smash the plate glass window)

The dead face is the true face
of Washington, New York a misery, but north and east
the carpenter obeyed
topography

As a hand addresses itself to the care of plants
and a sense of proportion, the house
is put to the earth

Tho peopled with hants, New England

Move over to let the death-blow in,
the unmanned or the transvest, drest
in beard and will, the capillary

Seven years with the wrong man,
7 yrs of tristus and vibullation.
And I looked up to see a toad. And the boy sd:
"I crushed one, and its blood is green"

Green, is the color of my true love's green
despite
New England is
despite her merchants and her morals

La Chute

my drum, hollowed out thru the thin slit,
carved from the cedar wood, the base I took
when the tree was felled

o my lute, wrought from the tree's crown

my drum, whose lustiness
was not to be resisted

                              my lute,
from whose pulsations
not one could turn away

                                    They
are where the dead are, my drum fell
where the dead are, who
will bring it up, my lute
who will bring it up where it fell in the face of them
where they are, where my lute and drum have fallen?

The Kingfishers

1

What does not change / is the will to change

He woke, fully clothed, in his bed. He
remembered only one thing, the birds, how
when he came in, he had gone around the rooms
and got them back in their cage, the green one first,
she with the bad leg, and then the blue,
the one they had hoped was a male

Otherwise? Yes, Fernand, who had talked lispingly of Albers & Angkor Vat.
He had left the party without a word. How he got up, got into his coat,
I do not know. When I saw him, he was at the door, but it did not matter,
he was already sliding along the wall of the night, losing himself
in some crack of the ruins. That it should have been he who said, "The kingfishers!
who cares
for their feathers
now?"

His last words had been, "The pool is slime." Suddenly everyone,
ceasing their talk, sat in a row around him, watched
they did not so much hear, or pay attention, they
wondered, looked at each other, smirked, but listened,
he repeated and repeated, could not go beyond his thought
"The pool   the kingfishers' feathers were wealth   why
did the export stop?"

It was then he left

2

I thought of the E on the stone, and of what Mao said
la lumiere"

> but the kingfisher

de l'aurore"

> but the kingfisher flew west

est devant nous!

> he got the color of his breast
> from the heat of the setting sun!

The features are, the feebleness of the feet (syndactylism of the 3rd & 4th digit)
the bill, serrated, sometimes a pronounced beak, the wings
where the color is, short and round, the tail
inconspicuous.

But not these things were the factors. Not the birds.
The legends are
legends. Dead, hung up indoors, the kingfisher
will not indicate a favoring wind,
or avert the thunderbolt. Nor, by its nesting,
still the waters, with the new year, for seven days.
It is true, it does nest with the opening year, but not on the waters.
It nests at the end of a tunnel bored by itself in a bank. There,
six or eight white and translucent eggs are laid, on fishbones
not on bare clay, on bones thrown up in pellets by the birds.

> On these rejectamenta

(as they accumulate they form a cup-shaped structure) the young are born.
And, as they are fed and grow, this nest of excrement and decayed fish becomes

> a dripping, fetid mass

Mao concluded:

> nous devons
>
> > nous lever
> >
> > > et agir!

3

When the attentions change / the jungle
leaps in

> even the stones are split
>
> > they rive

Or,
enter
that other conqueror we more naturally recognize
he so resembles ourselves

But the E
cut so rudely on that oldest stone
sounded otherwise,
was differently heard

as, in another time, were treasures used:

(and, later, much later, a fine ear thought
a scarlet coat)

> "of green feathers   feet, beaks and eyes
> of gold
>
> "animals likewise,
> resembling snails

"a large wheel, gold, with figures of unknown four-foots,
and worked with tufts of leaves, weight
3800 ounces

"last, two birds, of thread and featherwork, the quills
gold, the feet
gold, the two birds perched on two reeds
gold, the reeds arising from two embroidered mounds,
one yellow, the other
white.

"And from each reed hung
seven feathered tassels.

In this instance, the priests
(in dark cotton robes, and dirty,
their dishevelled hair matted with blood, and flowing wildly
over their shoulders)
rush in among the people, calling on them
to protect their gods

And all now is war
where so lately there was peace,
and the sweet brotherhood, the use
of tilled fields.

4

Not one death but many,
not accumulation but change, the feed-back proves, the feed-back is
the law

Into the same river no man steps twice
When fire dies air dies
No one remains, nor is, one

Around an appearance, one common model, we grow up
many. Else how is it,
if we remain the same,
we take pleasure now
in what we did not take pleasure before? love
contrary objects? admire and/or find fault? use
other words, feel other passions, have
nor figure, appearance, disposition, tissue
the same?
To be in different states without a change
is not a possibility

We can be precise. The factors are
in the animal and/or the machine the factors are
communication and/or control, both involve
the message. And what is the message? The message is
a discrete or continuous sequence of measurable events distributed in time

is the birth of air, is
the birth of water, is
a state between
the origin and
the end, between
birth and the beginning of
another fetid nest

is change, presents
no more than itself

And the too strong grasping of it,
when it is pressed together and condensed,
loses it

This very thing you are

II

      They buried their dead in a sitting posture
      serpent   cane   razor   ray of the sun

      And she sprinkled water on the head of the child, crying
      "Cioa-coatl! Cioa-coatl!"
      with her face to the west

      Where the bones are found, in each personal heap
      with what each enjoyed, there is always
      the Mongolian louse

The light is in the east. Yes. And we must rise, act. Yet
in the west, despite the apparent darkness (the whiteness
which covers all), if you look, if you can bear, if you can, long enough

      as long as it was necessary for him, my guide
      to look into the yellow of that longest-lasting rose

so you must, and, in that whiteness, into that face, with what candor, look

and, considering the dryness of the place
      the long absence of an adequate race

      (of the two who first came, each a conquistador, one healed, the other
      tore the eastern idols down, toppled
      the temple walls, which, says the excuser
      were black from human gore)

hear
hear, where the dry blood talks
    where the old appetite walks

                        la piu saporita et migliore
                        che si possa truovar al mondo

where it hides, look
in the eye how it runs
in the flesh / chalk

        but under these petals
        in the emptiness
        regard the light, contemplate
        the flower

whence it arose

        with what violence benevolence is bought
        what cost in gesture justice brings
        what wrongs domestic rights involve
        what stalks
        this silence

        what pudor pejorocracy affronts
        how awe, night-rest and neighborhood can rot
        what breeds where dirtiness is law
        what crawls
        below

III

        I am no Greek, hath not th'advantage.
        And of course, no Roman:

he can take no risk that matters,
the risk of beauty least of all.

But I have my kin, if for no other reason than
(as he said, next of kin) I commit myself, and,
given my freedom, I'd be a cad
if I didn't. Which is most true.

It works out this way, despite the disadvantage.
I offer, in explanation, a quote:
si j'ai du goût, ce n'est guères
que pour la terre et les pierres.

Despite the discrepancy (an ocean   courage   age)
this is also true: if I have any taste
it is only because I have interested myself
in what was slain in the sun

    I pose you your question:

shall you uncover honey / where maggots are?

    I hunt among stones

At Yorktown

1

At Yorktown the church

at Yorktown the dead

at Yorktown the grass

are live

        at York-town the earth

piles itself in shallows,

declares itself, like water,

by pools and mounds

2

At Yorktown the dead

are soil

at Yorktown the church

is marl

at Yorktown the swallows

dive where it is greenest,

        the hollows

are eyes are flowers, the heather,

equally accurate, is hands

at York-town only the flies

dawdle, like history,

in the sun

3

at Yorktown the earthworks

braw

at Yorktown the mortars

of brass, weathered green, of mermaids

for handles, of Latin

for texts, scream

without noise

like a gull

4

At Yorktown the long dead

loosen the earth, heels

sink in, over an abatis

a bird wheels

and time is a shine caught blue

from a martin's

back

In Cold Hell, in Thicket

In cold hell, in thicket, how
abstract (as high mind, as not lust, as love is) how
strong (as strut or wing, as polytope, as things are
constellated) how
strung, how cold
can a man stay (can men) confronted
thus?

All things are made bitter, words even
are made to taste like paper, wars get tossed up
like lead soldiers used to be
(in a child's attic) lined up
to be knocked down, as I am,
by firings from a spit-hardened fort, fronted
as we are, here, from where we must go

God, that man, as his acts must, as there is always
a thing he can do, he can raise himself, he raises
on a reed he raises his

Or, if it is me, what
he has to say

1

What has he to say?
In hell it is not easy
to know the traceries, the markings
(the canals, the pits, the mountings by which space
declares herself, arched, as she is, the sister,

awkward stars drawn for teats to pleasure him, the brother
who lies in stasis under her, at ease as any monarch or
a happy man

How shall he who is not happy, who has been so made unclear,
who is no longer privileged to be at ease, who, in this brush, stands
reluctant, imageless, unpleasured, caught in a sort of hell, how
shall he convert this underbrush, how turn this unbidden place
how trace and arch again
the necessary goddess?

2

The branches made against the sky are not of use, are
already done, like snow-flakes, do not, cannot service
him who has to raise   (Who puts this on, this damning of his flesh?)
he can, but how far, how sufficiently far can he raise the thickets of
this wilderness?

> How can he change, his question is
> these black and silvered knivings, these
> awkwardnesses?

> How can he make these blood-points into panels, into sides
> for a king's, for his own
> for a wagon, for a sleigh, for the beak of, the running sides of
> a vessel fit for
> moving?

> How can he make out, he asks,
> of this low eye-view,
> size?

And archings traced and picked enough to hold
to stay, as she does, as he, the brother, when,
here where the mud is, he is frozen, not daring
where the grass grows, to move his feet from fear
he'll trespass on his own dissolving bones, here
where there is altogether too much remembrance?

3

The question, the fear he raises up himself against
(against the same each act is proffered, under the eyes
each fix, the town of the earth over, is managed) is: Who
am I?

Who am I but by a fix, and another,
a particle, and the congery of particles carefully picked one by another,

        as in this thicket, each
        smallest branch, plant, fern, root
        —roots lie, on the surface, as nerves are laid open—
        must now (the bitterness of the taste of her) be
        isolated, observed, picked over, measured, raised
        as though a word, an accuracy were a pincer!
                                    this

            is the abstract, this
            is the cold doing, this
            is the almost impossible

So shall you blame those
who give it up, those who say
it isn't worth the struggle?

                  (Prayer

     Or a death as going over to—shot by yr own forces—to
     a greener place?

                      Neither

    any longer
    usable)

        By fixes only (not even any more by shamans)
        can the traceries
        be brought out

      II

ya, selva oscura, but hell now
is not exterior, is not to be got out of, is
the coat of your own self, the beasts
emblazoned on you   And who
can turn this total thing, invert
and let the ragged sleeves be seen
by any bitch or common character?   Who
can endure it where it is, where the beasts are met,
where yourself is, your beloved is, where she
who is separate from you, is not separate, is not
goddess, is, as your core is,
the making of one hell

          where she moves off, where she is
          no longer arch

     (this is why he of whom we speak does not move, why
     he stands so awkward where he is, why
     his feet are held, like some ragged crane's

off the nearest next ground, even from
the beauty of the rotting fern his eye
knows, as he looks down, as,
in utmost pain if cold can be so called,
he looks around this battlefield, this
rotted place where men did die, where boys
and immigrants have fallen, where nature
(the years that she's took over)
does not matter, where

      that men killed, do kill, that woman kills
      is part, too, of his question

2

That it is simple, what the difference is—
that a man, men, are now their own wood
and thus their own hell and paradise
that they are, in hell or in happiness, merely
something to be wrought, to be shaped, to be carved, for use, for
others

does not in the least lessen his, this unhappy man's
obscurities, his
confrontations

He shall step, he
will shape, he
is already also
moving off

      into the soil, on to his own bones

he will cross

> (there is always a field,
> for the strong there is always
> an alternative)

>> But a field
> is not a choice, is
> as dangerous as a prayer, as a death, as any
> misleading, lady

He will cross

> And is bound to enter (as she is)
> a later wilderness.
>> Yet
> what he does here, what he raises up
> (he must, the stakes are such

>>>> this at least
> is a certainty, this
> is a law, is not one of the questions, this
> is what was talked of as
> —what was it called, demand?)

He will do what he now does, as she will, do
carefully, do
without wavering,
without

> as even the branches,
> even in this dark place, the twigs

>>>> how

> even the brow
of what was once to him a beautiful face

as even the snow-flakes waver in the light's eye

     as even forever wavers (gutters
     in the wind of loss)

     even as he will forever waver

     precise as hell is, precise
     as any words, or wagon,
     can be made

For Sappho, Back

I

With a dry eye, she
saw things out of the corner of,
with a bold
she looked on any man,
with a shy eye

With a cold eye, with her eye she looked on, she looked out, she
who was not so different as you might imagine from,
who had, as nature hath, an eye to look upon her makings, to,
in her womb, know
how red, and because it is red, how
handsome blood is, how, because it is unseen, how
because it goes about its business as she does,
as nature's things have that way of doing, as
in the delight of her eye she
creates constants

                        And, in the thickness of her blood, some
variants

II

As blood is, as flesh can be
is she, self-housed, and moving
moving in impeccability to be
clear, clear! to be
as, what is rhythm but
her limpidity?
               She

who is as certain as the morning is
when it arises, when it is spring, when, from wetness comes its brightness
as fresh as this beloved's fingers, lips
each new time she new turns herself to
tendernesses, she
turns her most objective, scrupulous attention, her own
self-causing

   each time it is,
   as is the morning, is
   the morning night and revelation of her
   nakednesses, new
   forever new, as fresh as is the scruple of her eye, the accurate
   kiss

III

If you would know what woman is, what
strength the reed of man unknows, forever
cannot know, look, look! in these eyes, look
as she passes, on this moving thing, which moves
as grass blade by grass blade moves, as
syllable does throw light on fellow syllable, as,
in this rare creature, each hidden, each moving thing
is light to its known, unknown brother,
as objects stand one by one by another, so
is this universe, this flow, this woman, these eyes
are sign

IV

The intimate, the intricate, what shall perplex, forever
is a matter, is it not, not of confusions to be studied and made literal,
but of a dry dance by which, as shoots one day make leaves, as
the earth's crust, when ice draws back, wrings mountains
from itself, makes valleys in whose palms
root-eating fisher folk spring up—
by such a dance, in which the dancer contradicts
the waste and easy gesture, contains
the heave within,
within, because the human is so light a structure, within
a finger, say, or there
within the gentlest swaying of

           (of your true hips)

In such containment

        And in search for that which is the shoot, the thrust
of what you are

      (of what you were so delicately born)

                of what fruits
of your own making you are

        the hidden constance of which all the rest
is awkward variation

      this! this
      is what gives beauty to her eye, inhabitation
      to her tender-taken bones, is what illumines
      all her skin with satin glow
      when love blows over, turning

as the leaf turns in the wind
and, with that shock of recognition, shows
its other side, the joy, the sort of terror of

a dancer going off

The Moon Is the Number 18

is a monstrance,
the blue dogs bay,
and the son sits,
grieving

is a grinning god, is
the mouth of, is
the dripping moon

while in the tower the cat
preens
and all motion
is a crab

and there is nothing he can do but what they do, watch
the face of waters, and fire

      The blue dogs paw,
      lick the droppings, dew
      or blood, whatever
      results are. And night,
      the crab, rays round
      attentive as the cat to catch
      human sound

      The blue dogs rue,
      as he does, as he would howl, confronting
      the wind which rocks what was her, while prayers
      striate the snow, words blow

        as questions cross fast, fast
        as flames, as flames form, melt
        along any darkness

Birth is an instance as is a host, namely, death

The moon has no air

        In the red tower
        in that tower where she also sat
        in that particular tower where watching & moving are,
        there,
        there where what triumph there is, is: there
        is all substance, all creature
        all there is against the dirty moon, against
        number, image, sortilege—

        alone with cat & crab,
        and sound is, is, his
        conjecture

To Gerhardt, There, Among Europe's
Things of Which He Has Written Us
in His "Brief an Creeley und Olson"

so pawed,
by this long last Bear-son

    with no crockery broken,
    but no smile in my mouth

        June 28th, '51, on this horst
        on the Heat Equator, a mediterranean sea
        to the east, and north
        what saves America from desert, waters
        and thus rain-bearing winds,
        by subsidence, salt-waters
           (by which they came,
           the whelps, looking
           for youth

Which they found.
        And have continuously sought
                  to kill

        (o Old Man,
    in winter, when before me, cross my path

    in summer, when behind me, cross my path

If you want to shut yourself in, shut yourself in
If you do not want to shut yourself in, come out

> A zoo
> is what he's come to, the old
> Beginner, the old
> Winner

Who took all,
for awhile

> (My grandfather, my grandmother,
> why have you died?
> Did a hand to hand struggle come?
> Did a war, the size of a man's fist come?)

1

The proposition, Gerhardt
is to get it straight, right
from the start.

> Help raise the bones
> of the great man.
>
> Meat and bones we won't throw away.
> We pile it up in a lonely place.
>
> We do not throw on the ground.
> Your meat and bones without purpose.
> We take bones and meat.
>
> O Grandfather,
> you went to war

The first duty is
to knock out his teeth, saying
"These are the teeth with which you devour all animals."

I offer you no proper names
either from great cities
on the other side of civilization
which have only to be visited
to be got the hell out of, by bus
or motorcycle, simply because place
as a force is a lie,
or at most a small truth,
now that man has no oar to screw down into the earth, and say
here i'll plant, does not know
why he should cease
staying on the prowl

> You climbed up the tree after some foul berry
> and fell down and died
> You ate berries, fell from the rock
> and died
> You ate sorb berries
> and died
> You ate raspberries,
> drowned in the swamp and died

Or from the other side of time, from a time on the other side of yourself
from which you have so lightly borrowed men, naming them as though,
like your litany of Europe's places, you could take up
their power: magic, my light-fingered faust,
is not so easily sympathetic. Nor are the ladies
worn so decoratively.

The top of the spring plant
noisily chewing

The top of the summer plant
noisily chewing

On a summer day walk before and behind me
on a winter day

2

Nor can I talk of method, in the face of your letter,
in verse or otherwise,
as though it were a dance
of rains, or schmerz, of words as signs worn
like a toupee on the head of a Poe cast
in plaster, any method otherwise than
he practised it who gave it up,
after a summer in his mother's barn,
because the place smelled so, because time
his time, precisely this now
And with no back references, no
floating over Asia arrogating
how a raiding party moves in advance of a nation thereby
eventually
giving a language the international power
poets take advantage of. As they also,
with much less reason, from too much economics speak
of the dream
in a peasant's bent shoulders, as though it were true
they cared a damn
for his conversation

On a mountain with dry stalks, walk
with a resounding tread

On a mountain with meadow-sweet
walk with a resounding tread

On the way to your fathers,
join them

3

Nor of a film, or of strange birds,
or of ordinary ones. Nor with the power of American vocables
would I arm you in Kansas, when you come,
or there, if you have to stay, where you feel so strongly
the dead center of the top of time

          I am giving you a present

          I am giving you a present

For you forget (forgetting
is much more your problem
than you know, right-handed one
who so beautifully reminds me
that the birds stand
in the middle of the air
and that always, in that apsed place
in which so many have kneeled
as I do not have the soul to kneel, the fields
are forever harvested, and happy heaven
leans over backwards

to pour its blessings by downfall
on to black earth

Admitting that among the ruins
    with a like schmerz in every vessel of his throat,
    he repeated, "Among the ruins, among them
    the finest memory in the Orient"
one will go about picking up old pieces
    bric-a-brac, he snorted, who did not know whereof he spoke,
    he had so allowed himself to be removed, to back-trail
or put it immediately out of the mind, as some can,
stuff the construction hole quickly with a skyscraper

but you will remember that even Caesar comes to this, certainly you
who has written of Hamlet's death, who is able to handle such large counters
as the classic poet handled bank-notes in our time, before prizes
were his lot, and I am envious, who can do neither

that the point of the rotting of man in his place is also
(beside the long-lived earth of good farmers, its manuring,
what Duncan pointed out America and Russia are very careless with)
what blows about and blocks a hole where the wind was used to go

        (While walking on the earth with stalks
        you received a present

        While walking on the earth with the stalks of plants
        your head was crushed

        You could not see, your eyes got small,
        you could not defecate, you were small
        you could not,
        therefore you died

It is a rod of mountain ash I give you, Rainer Maria Gerhardt,
instead of any other thing, in order that you may also be
left-handed, as he was, your Grandfather,
whom you have all forgotten, have even lost the song of, how
he was to be addressed:

> "Great man,
>   in climbing up the tree,
>   broke his leg."

I am urging you from here
where nothing is brutal,
not even the old economics
>   (I do not dare to breathe
>   for what I know the new
>   will do) and only the kids kill
frigate-birds, because they have to
to develop a throwing arm

>   (as your people knew, if I can lead you
>   to go back far enough,
>   which is not one step from where you are

>> "His ear is the earth.
>>   Let you be careful"

>   that he must be hunted, that to eat
>   you shall bring him down

>> "Your head
>>   is the size of a ladle

>> Your soul
>>   is of the size of a thread

Do not enter my soul by day,
do not enter my dreams by night

that woman—who is, with more resistance
than you seem to have allowed, named—
lends herself to him as concubine

what you forget is, you

are their son! You are not

Telemachus. And that you come back

under your own

steam

There are no broken stones, no statues, no images, phrases, composition
otherwise than
what Creeley and I also have,
and without reference to
what reigned in the house
and is now well dismissed

Let you pray to him, we say
who are without such fatherhood:

"Show your house in spring.

Show a mound of snow in your house in winter.

In summer go in back of and in front of
the children.

Think not badly of the man, go right."

4

Or come here
where we will welcome you
with nothing but what is, with
no useful allusions, with no birds
but those we stone, nothing to eat
but ourselves, no end and no beginning, I assure you, yet
not at all primitive, living as we do in a space we do not need to contrive

And with the predecessors who, though they are not our nouns, the verbs
are like!

So we are possessed of what you cry over, time
and magic numbers

     Language,
     my enemie,
     is no such system:

          "Hey, old man, the war arrived.

          Be still, old man.

          Your mouth is shut,

          your door is shut,"

As I said, I am giving you a present.
To all false dimensions,
including his superb one
who refused to allow the social question in,
to all such fathers and false girls
(one of his, I notice, you take, seriously)
why not say what, somewhere, you must hear the echo of?

"One eye
sees heaven,
another eye
sees earth

For the problem is one of focus, of the field as well as the point of
vision: you will solve your problem best
without displacement

"One ear
hears heaven,
another ear
hears earth."

In such simplicities I would have you address me,
another time

5

The old man, my grandfather, died.
The old woman, my grandmother, died.
And now my father visits me, clothed
in a face he never wore, with an odor
I do not know as his, as his was meadow-sweet.
He sits, grieving, that she should have worried,
and I look up at him as he sits there
and if I am his son, this man
is from as far a place and time
as yours is, carries with him
the strangeness you and I will carry
for our sons, and for like reason,
that we are such that can be pawed

"We are no murderers," they used so carefully to say.

"We have put in order the bones of him
  whom others kill."

You see, we are experienced of what you speak of: silence
with no covering of ashes, geraniums also
and loaded with aphis

                  of all but war,

but war, too, is dead as the lotus is dead

                  And our hardness

has been exaggerated. You see,
we see nothing downward: we walk, as your grandfather walked,
without looking at his feet

                "And because of meeting the great man,
                  a feast is held

                Warm yourself,
                over the fire of grandfather

                This is an offering to the guests, a holiday
                of the great man

                He will feel satisfied

                He will not take revenge

The stick is a reminder, Gerhardt. And the song? what seems
to have been forgotten?

Here it is (as we say here, in our anti-cultural speech, made up
of particulars only, which we don't, somehow, confuse with gossip:

"To his resting place in spring,

to his house in autumn,

I shall go

With autumn plant, arouse the mountain

With spring plant, arouse the mountain

In summer, walk in the background,
do not frighten the children,
do not sniff, neither here
nor there."

The Ring of

it was the west wind caught her up, as
she rose
from the genital
wave, and bore her from the delicate
foam, home
to her isle

and those lovers
of the difficult, the hours
of the golden day welcomed her, clad her, were
as though they had made her, were wild
to bring this new thing born
of the ring of the sea pink
& naked, this girl, brought her
to the face of the gods, violets
in her hair

Beauty, and she
said no to zeus & them all, all were not or
was it she chose the ugliest
to bed with, or was it straight
and to expiate the nature of beauty, was it?

knowing hours, anyway,
she did not stay long, or the lame
was only one part, & the handsome
mars had her   And the child
had that name, the arrow of

as the flight of, the move of
his mother who adorneth

with myrtle the dolphin and words
they rise, they do who
are born of like
elements

An Ode on Nativity

I

All cries rise, & the three of us
observe how fast Orion
marks midnight
at the climax
of the sky
     while the boat of the moon settles
as red in the southwest
as the orb of her was, for this boy, once,
the first time he saw her whole halloween face northeast
across the skating pond as he came down to the ice, December
his seventh year.
     Winter, in this zone,
is an off & on thing, where the air
is sometimes as shining as ice is
when the sky's lights . . . When the ducks
are the only skaters
    And a crèche
is a commerciality

    (The same year, a ball of fire
    the same place—exactly through
    the same trees
    was fire:

       the Sawyer lumber company yard
       was a moon of pain, at the end of itself,
       and the death of horses I saw burning,
       fallen through the floors

                              into the buried Blackstone River the city
                              had hidden under itself, had grown over

               At any time, & this time
               a city
jangles

               Man's splendor
is a question of which
birth

II

The cries rise, & one of us
has not even eyes to see the night's sky
burning, or the hollows
made coves of mist & frost, the barns
covered over, and nothing in the night but two of us
following the blind highway to catch all glimpses
of the settling, rocking moon

                    December, in this year
is a new thing, where I whisper
bye-low, and the pond
is full to its shores again, so full
I read the moon where grass would not reveal it
a month ago, and the ducks make noises
like my daughter does, stir
in the crèche of things

                    (His mother, 80, and we
                    ate oysters after the burial: we had knelt
                    with his sister, now Mary Josephine,

in the prayery of the convent of the church
where my mother & father had been married

And she told us tales of my family
I had not heard, how my grandfather
rolled wild in the green grass
on the banks of that same now underground river
to cool himself from the steel mill's fires
stripped down to his red underwear

she was that gay, to have seen her daughter
and that the two of us had had that car
to take the Sisters downtown and drop them
where they had to go

                    I had watched them
swirl off in their black habits
before I started the car again
in the snow of that street, the same street
my father had taken me to, to buy my first cap

At any time, & now, again, in this new year
the place of your birth, even a city, rings

in & out of
tune

What shall be
my daughter's second
birth?

III

All things now rise, and the cries of men to be born
in ways afresh, aside from all old narratives, away
from intervals too wide to mark the grasses

> (not those on which cattle feed, or single stars
> which show the way to buy bad goods
> in green & red lit stores, no symbols

the grasses in the ice, or Orion's sweep, or
the closeness of turning snows, these
can tell the tale of any one of us stormed or quieted
by our own things, what belong, tenaciously,
to our own selves

> Any season, in this fresh time
is off & on to that degree that any of us miss
the vision, lose the instant and decision, the close
which can be nothing more and no thing else
than that which unborn form you are the content of, which you
alone can make to shine, throw that like light
even where the mud was and now there is a surface
ducks, at least, can walk on. And I
have company
in the night

> In this year, in this time
> when spirits do not walk abroad, when men alone walk
>
> when to walk is so difficult
>
> when the divine tempter also walks
> renewing his offer—that choice

                                   (to turn
            from the gross fire, to hide
            as that boy almost did, to bury himself
            from the fearful face—twice!—that winter

            to roll like a dog or his grandfather
            in the snowbank on the edge of the pond's ice

            to find comfort somewhere, to avoid
            the burning—To go to grass
            as his daughter now suckles. Some way! he cries out
            not to see those horses' agonies:

                     Is light, is there any light, any
                     to pay the price of
                     fire?

IV

The question stays
in the city out of tune, the skies
not seen, now, again, in
a bare winter time:

             is there any birth
any other splendor than
the brilliance of the going on, the loneliness
whence all our cries arise?

The Thing Was Moving

It's so beautiful, life, goddamn death
that we have to die, only the mind knows
what lies next the heart or a five-petaled flower
restores the fringed gentians I used to so love
I'd lie amongst them in the meadow near the house
which was later covered by a dump to make an athletic field
and the brook was gone to which we tried to speed our sleds
from the hill the house stood on and which the dump
was meant to join, the loss punctuated by the shooting
my father taught me with the rifle he gave me from the back porch
of the three-decker, the rats living among the cans and peat
as the dump came closer, and I hated
all of it (the same porch the chameleon he had bought me
escaped from, from the cage I'd made it
of old screen when we brought it home from the circus

the smoke from the dump-fires all the time the thing was moving
toward us, covering the meadow, coming from the hill
(where we had had the single cable swing had broke
that day i was alone there and i had flown
out over all that space, and my glasses
beyond me, and my back to this day . . . and i groping
not to tell my parents, and to find the glasses
to find my way back. The fire-engines
in the evening dousing—and no flames but the littlest, all
smoke turning into steam there, but the excitement . . .

the concrete sections, when the dump began to reach
the brook, to put it under, like hoops we could not roll
in which—they were so high—we lost ourselves
like tunnels, or took it we were five-figured forms
fit to fill a circle and be acrobats, our heads
wedged but no movement of those sections even
when we pried them and were unknowingly in such danger
as when we built the club-house of railroad ties
on the edge of another flat, the swamp where the man
and his horse and team went down in the quicksand, and we
did not know until after the cops had broken down the structure
and even later when the auto showrooms covered it, and piles
had to be driven . . . the hunting, of each other, before the brook
was let in and only way above, or below at Chandler Street
was it any more where I had sunk in, where the irises were,
where I had seen my first turtle, or further up, where
girls had swum naked that day I had tittupped
from the piano lesson, seeking my friends, and suddenly,
coming on the pool, had heard the voices first, and slowed
so that I saw them from the bushes (the older woman
turning me back . . . the invasion

or the ford (below Dick Marsden's house) horses crossed
and we sailed boats, or made dams, the wonder
of the way the hill sloped up there, the gradual way
before it became a suburb and was still the West
(the trench we were sure had been emplacements
of King Phillip's Wars ended before the ford, before
the whole brook system got transverse to what it was below
near where I lived, Hill's Farm getting its fields

from the change of the direction of its flow,
and the topography
                              the flowers (as well as the ball field)
were located, in my space, by this curving
from west to south, the farm marking the change
and running against the foot of my house, the brick wall
on which all the wood stood which shook
when the wind bellied down that valley and struck
the broad back of the house and I used to think
why the whipping of the house on that third-floor
didn't throw it down, and only that the storm
was not like marching men on a bridge, was out of step
was irregular as men are, and as multiple, the times we are
and our materials are so much more numerous
than any such thing as the heart's flow
or the sun's coming up, why
man is man's delight, and there is no backward
except his, how far it goes, as far
as any thing he's made, dug up or lighted
by a flare in some such cave as I never knew
except as that concrete hid my brook and I was as large
(before they put the pieces in below ground) inside any one hoop
as any pentamerous thing, this figwort
which provokes me
and I study
bract thallus involucre whorl
of all my life, of torus I am, holding
all I shall be, hungry

that it should never end, that my throat
which has no longer thymus and all that went with it
might speak forever the glory of
what it is to live, so bashful as man is
bare

Merce of Egypt

1 I sing the tree is a heron
    I praise long grass.
    I wear the lion skin
    over the long skirt
    to the ankle. The ankle
    is a heron

    I look straightly backward. Or I bend to the side straightly
    to raise the sheaf
    up the stick of the leg
    as the bittern's leg, raised
    as slow as
    his neck grows
    as the wheat. The presentation,
    the representation,
    is flat

    I am followed by women and a small boy in white carrying a duck,
    all have flat feet and, foot before foot, the women with black wigs
    And I intent
    upon idlers,
    and flowers

2   the sedge
    as tall as I am, the rushes
    as I am

        as far as I am animal, antelope
    with such's attendant carnivores

                                    and rows of beaters
drive the game to the hunter, or into nets,
where it is thick-wooded or there are open spaces
with low shrubs

3 I speak downfall, the ball of my foot
   on the neck of the earth, the hardsong
   of the rise of all trees, the jay
   who uses the air. I am the recovered sickle
   with the grass-stains still on the flint of its teeth.
   I am the six-rowed barley
   they cut down.

   I am tree. The boy of the back of my legs
   is roots. I am water fowl
   when motion is the season of my river, and the wild boar
   casts me. But my time
   is hawkweed,

4 I hold what the wind blows, and silt.
   I hide in the swamps of the valley to escape civil war,
   and marauding soldiers. In the new procession
   I am first, and carry wine
   made of dandelions. The new rites
   are my bones

   I built my first settlement
   in groves

5   as they would flail crops
     when the spring comes, and flood, the tassels
     rise, as my head

The Death of Europe

(a funeral poem for Rainer M. Gerhardt)

Rainer,
the man who was about to celebrate his 52nd birthday
the day I learned of your death at 28, said:
"I lie out on Dionysius' tongue"!

the sort of language you talked, and I did,
correctly—
                as I heard this other German wrongly,
from his accent, and because I was thinking of you,
talking of how much you gave us all hearing
in Germany (as I watch a salamander on the end of a dead pine branch
snagging flies), what I heard this man almost twice your age say was,
"I lie out on a dinosaur's tongue"!

for my sense, still, is that,
despite your sophistication
and your immense labors . . .

It will take some telling. It has to do with what WCW
(of all that you published in *fragmente*, to see Bill's
R R BUMS in futura!

                it has to do with how far back are

Americans
as well as,
Germans

            "walk on spongey feet
            if you would cross

carry purslane
if you get into her bed

guard the changes
when you scratch your ear

I

It is this business
that you should die!
Who shot up,
out of the ruins,
and hung there,
in the sky,
the first of Europe
I could have words with:

as Holderlin on Patmos you
trying to hold bay leaves
on a cinder block!

Now I can only console you,
sing of willows,
and dead branches,
worry the meanness
that you do not live,
wear the ashes
of loss

Neither of us
carrying a stick
any more

Creeley told me
how you lived

II

I have urged anyone
back (as Williams asked
that Sam Houston
be recognized
                as I said,
Rainer, plant
your ash

        "I drive a stake into the ground, isn't it silly,"
I said out loud in the night, "to drive a stake into the ground?"

How primitive
does one have to get? Or,

as you and I were both open
to the charge: how large

can a quote

get, he

said, eyeing me

with a blue

eye

                Were your eyes

                brown, Rainer?

Rainer,

who is in the ground,

what did you look like?

Did you die of your head bursting

like a land-mine?

Did you walk

on your own unplanted self?

III

It is not hell you came into,
or came out of. It is not moly
any of us are given. It is merely
that we are possessed of
the irascible. We are blind
not from the darkness
but by creation we are
moles. We are let out
sightless, and thus miss
what we are given, what woman
is, what your two sons
looking out of a picture at me,
sitting on some small hillside—

they have brown eyes, surely.

Rainer, the thyrsus
is down

I can no longer
put anything
into your hands

It does no good
for me to wish
to arm you

I can only carry laurel,
and some red flowers,
mere memorials, not cut
with my own knife an oar
for you, last poet
of a civilization

You are nowhere
but in the ground

IV

What breaks my heart
is that your grandfather
did not do better, that our grandmothers
(I think we agreed)
did not tell us
the proper tales

so that we are as raw
as our inventions, have not the teeth
to bite off Grandfather's
paws

(O, Rainer,
you should have ridden your bike
across the Atlantic instead of your mind,
that bothered itself too much
with how we were hanging on
to the horse's tail, fared, fared
we who had Sam Houston, not
Ulysses

> I can only cry: Those
> who gave you not enough
> caused you to settle for
> too little

> The ground
> is now the sky

V

But even Bill
is not protected,
no swift messenger
puts pussley
even in his hand,
open,

as it is, no one says how
to eat
at the hairy table

            (as your scalp
also lifted,

as your ears

did not stay

silk

        O my collapsed brother,
the body
does bring us
down
        The images
have to be
contradicted
           The metamorphoses
are to be
undone

The stick,
and the ear

are to be no more than

they are: the cedar

and the lebanon

of this impossible

life.

I give you no visit

to your mother.

What you have left us

is what you did

It is enough

It is what we

praise

I take back

the stick.

I open my hand

to throw dirt

into your grave

I praise you

who watched the riding

on the horse's back

It was your glory to know

that we must mount

O that the Earth

had to be given to you

this way!

O Rainer, rest

in the false

peace

Let us who live

try

A Newly Discovered 'Homeric' Hymn

(for Jane Harrison, if she were alive)

Hail and beware the dead who will talk life until you are blue
in the face. And you will not understand what is wrong,
they will not be blue, they will have tears in their eyes,
they will seem to you so much more full of life
than the rest of us, and they will ask so much, not of you no
but of life, they will cry, isn't it this way, if it isn't
I don't care for it, and you will feel the blackmail, you will not know
what to answer, it will all have become one mass

Hail and beware them, for they come from where you have not been,
they come from where you cannot have come, they come into life
by a different gate. They come from a place which is not easily known,
it is known only to those who have died. They carry seeds
you must not touch, you must not touch the pot they taste of,
no one must touch the pot, no one must, in their season.

Hail and beware them, in their season. Take care. Prepare
to receive them, they carry what the living cannot do without,
but take the proper precautions, do the prescribed things, let
down the thread from the right shoulder. And from the forehead.
And listen to what they say, listen to the talk, hear
every word of it—they are drunk from the pot, they speak
like no living man may speak, they have the seeds in their mouth—
listen, and beware

Hail them solely that they have the seeds in their mouth, they
are drunk, you cannot do without a drunkenness, seeds can't,
they must be soaked in the contents of the pot, they must be all one mass.
But you who live cannot know what else the seeds must be. Hail

and beware the earth, where the dead come from. Life
is not of the earth. The dead are of the earth. Hail and beware
the earth, where the pot is buried.

Greet the dead in the dead man's time. He is drunk of the pot.
He speaks like spring does. He will deceive you. You are meant
to be deceived. You must observe the drunkenness. You are not to
drink. But you must hear, and see. You must beware.

Hail them, and fall off. Fall off! The drink is not yours,
it is not yours! You do not come
from the same place, you do not suffer as the dead do,
they do not suffer, they need, because they have drunk of the pot,
they need. Do not drink of the pot, do not touch it. Do not touch
them.

Beware the dead. And hail them. They teach you drunkenness.
You have your own place to drink. Hail and beware them, when they come.

The chain of memory is resurrection   I am a vain man
I am interested in the size of the brain-case
of CroMagnon man and that his descendants are Guanches
right now in the Canary Islands, and that my father & mother
lie buried beside each other in the Swedish cemetery
in Worcester, Massachusetts. And my grandmother too.
Even if the Hineses are in St John's cemetery. Those stones
speak to me, my ear is their sea-shell as in Marin County
the big trees as well as the eucalyptus hold sounds
of Asia and Indians the myrtle, comes from Australia

The vector of space is resurrection. We walk on the earth
under which they lie who also matter to us, as well as those
who are distant, from whom we have got separated (as we are
separated from those we have not yet known: the loveliness
of man, that he shoots up men suddenly on the horizon
there is a new person who speaks as Ed Marshall does

and all the back country, the roads I have ridden
without headlights the moon was so bright on the houses
and I was coming from a love in Lawrence, and Georgetown
Rowley Ipswich lay out in the night, not blank at all as
now that Marshall has spoken, all the faces
and the stones
and Concord Avenue

rise into being: the onslaught,

he calls it,

resurrection

The being of man is resurrection, the genetic flow

of each life which has given life, the tenderness

none of us

is without. Let it come back. Let it be

where it is:

>"My soul is Chichester and my origin
>
>is a womb whether one likes it or not."

My ugliness,

said Juan Belmonte—to every Spaniard

I was part of himself:

>the bull (or whether he's a lion
>
>or a horse or the great snake)
>
>hammers us, mine beat me against
>
>the brick wall until I thought
>
>this is it, and it was only a redheaded boy
>
>diverted him

Direction—a directed magnitude—is

resurrection

>All that has been
>
>suddenly is: time

is the face

of recognition, Rhoda Straw; or my son

is a Magyar. The luminousness

of my daughter

to her mother

by a stream:

      apocatastasis

how it occurs, that in this instant I seek to speak

as though the species were a weed-seed a grass a barley corn

in the cup of my palm. And I was trying

to hear what it said, I was putting my heart down

to catch the pain

      Resurrection

is. It is the avowal. It is the admission. The renewal

is the restoration: the man in the dark with the animal

fat lamp

is my father. Or my grandfather. And the fat lady

who was weak from a heart attack and her granddaughter

I used to see courtin the boy on the motorcycle,

is my mother. Or my grandmother. The Venus

of Willendorf. We move

between two horns, the gate

of horn. And the animal or snake who warns us

propels: we must woo the thing

to get its feet together so that its shoulder blades

are open, so that the aorta

One of the horns

is resurrection, the other horn

is any one of us: a river

is my sword, the Annisquam is my metal

you will have yours (a meadow his was, gone,

boy, in the dance and another

had a tree or there was a third

had a bicycle seat, and the face of all women,

he said,

they sat on. Bless the powers

that be

　　　This is a poem of celebration of the powers that be.

The large theme

is the smallest (the thumbtack

in the way of the inkbottle, the incident

which does not change the course even if the surface

of the day is changed because a hand followed a diaper

into the wringer up to the elbow, the smallest content

is a grit of occasion, the irrelevant

is only known

like the shape of the soul

to the person involved, the absolutes

sit in the palm of the hand which can't close

from the pain. I do not know

what you know at the same time that I do. My vanity

is only the exercise

of my privilege as yours, conceivably,

might be as hers, the peahen, is

also brilliant when she takes it up: Willendorf,

the stone, breathes back

into life. The resurrection

at the farthest point, and

        out of the green poison

        now the death of spring the jungle

        is in the gulley the growth

        has gone to the tropics small spring

        is over

        small spring

           while where my river flows

        spring is long. Here where the ice

        and the jungle once were identical

        spring is small

        the blossoms

        are already gone green green

        the worst green

        like paint floods

        the sky

        is like a bedroom wall

        in a motel

the horrors

of season too fast.

Without resurrection

all is too fast. The trees

crawl over everything like facts

like the fascination of irrelevant

events: to hew

o the dirty summer too early

for a man to catch up with

spring is dead! spring the horn

is dead. I Adonis

Lift me, life of being

I lift

the shape of my soul. In the face of spring

gone

into the growth

as the body was burned

on the sticks and went up

as smoke into the pale sky

o father

o mother

put into the ground

(o the beloved ones

they must dance

the thick green
which covers us, the appetite of nature
we stand off, the loss
of loss

In the chain of being
we arise, we make sparse
the virid covering, we lay bare
the dead, the winter ground, the snow
which makes the forsythia first
the first blossom

and in the two weeks of spring:
damn the green growth gone
to green bloom, the resurrection
is sparse   Desire
is spare   The confusion

of physical enjoyment
and desire   Desire

is resurrection

The soul
is an onslaught

As the Dead Prey Upon Us

As the dead prey upon us,
they are the dead in ourselves,
awake, my sleeping ones, I cry out to you,
disentangle the nets of being!

I pushed my car, it had been sitting so long unused.
I thought the tires looked as though they only needed air.
But suddenly the huge underbody was above me, and the rear tires
were masses of rubber and thread variously clinging together

as were the dead souls in the living room, gathered
about my mother, some of them taking care to pass
beneath the beam of the movie projector, some record
playing on the victrola, and all of them
desperate with the tawdriness of their life in hell

I turned to the young man on my right and asked, "How is it,
there?" And he begged me protestingly don't ask, we are poor
poor. And the whole room was suddenly posters and presentations
of brake linings and other automotive accessories, cardboard
displays, the dead roaming from one to another
as bored back in life as they are in hell, poor and doomed
to mere equipments

                        my mother, as alive as ever she was, asleep
when I entered the house as I often found her in a rocker
under the lamp, and awaking, as I came up to her, as she ever had

I found out she returns to the house once a week, and with her
the throng of the unknown young who center on her as much in death
as other like suited and dressed people did in life

O the dead!

> and the Indian woman and I
> enabled the blue deer
> to walk
>
> and the blue deer talked,
> in the next room,
> a Negro talk
>
> it was like walking a jackass,
> and its talk
> was the pressing gabber of gammers
> of old women
>
> and we helped walk it around the room
> because it was seeking socks
> or shoes for its hooves
> now that it was acquiring
>
> human possibilities

In the five hindrances men and angels
stay caught in the net, in the immense nets
which spread out across each plane of being, the multiple nets
which hamper at each step of the ladders as the angels
and the demons
and men
go up and down

> Walk the jackass
> Hear the victrola
> Let the automobile

be tucked into a corner of the white fence
when it is a white chair. Purity

is only an instant of being, the trammels

recur

In the five hindrances, perfection
is hidden

I shall get
to the place
10 minutes late.

It will be 20 minutes
of 9. And I don't know,

without the car,

how I shall get there

O peace, my mother, I do not know
how differently I could have done
what I did or did not do.

That you are back each week
that you fall asleep
with your face to the right

that you are as present there
when I come in as you were
when you were alive

that you are as solid, and your flesh
is as I knew it, that you have the company
I am used to your having

but o, that you all find it
such a cheapness!

o peace, mother, for the mammothness
of the comings and goings
of the ladders of life

The nets we are entangled in. Awake,
my soul, let the power into the last wrinkle
of being, let none of the threads and rubber of the tires
be left upon the earth. Let even your mother
go. Let there be only paradise

The desperateness is, that the instant
which is also paradise (paradise
is happiness) dissolves
into the next instant, and power
flows to meet the next occurrence

Is it any wonder
my mother comes back?
Do not that throng
rightly seek the room
where they might expect
happiness? They did not complain
of life, they obviously wanted
the movie, each other, merely to pass
among each other there,

where the real is, even to the display cards,
to be out of hell

The poverty
of hell

O souls, in life and in death,
awake, even as you sleep, even in sleep
know what wind
even under the crankcase of the ugly automobile
lifts it away, clears the sodden weights of goods,
equipment, entertainment, the foods the Indian woman,
the filthy blue deer, the 4 by 3 foot 'Viewbook,'
the heaviness of the old house, the stuffed inner room
lifts the sodden nets

> and they disappear as ghosts do,
> as spider webs, nothing
> before the hand of man

> The vent! You must have the vent,
> or you shall die. Which means
> never to die, the ghastliness

> of going, and forever
> coming back, returning
> to the instants which were not lived

> O mother, this I could not have done,
> I could not have lived what you didn't,
> I am myself netted in my own being

I want to die. I want to make that instant, too,
perfect

O my soul, slip
the cog

II

The death in life (death itself)
is endless, eternity
is the false cause

The knot is other wise, each topological corner
presents itself, and no sword
cuts it, each knot is itself its fire

each knot of which the net is made
is for the hands to untake
the knot's making. And touch alone

can turn the knot into its own flame

               (o mother, if you had once touched me

               o mother, if I had once touched you)

The car did not burn. Its underside
was not presented to me
a grotesque corpse. The old man

merely removed it as I looked up at it,
and put it in a corner of the picket fence
like was it my mother's white dog?

or a child's chair

The woman,
playing on the grass,
with her son (the woman next door)

was angry with me whatever it was
slipped across the playpen or whatever
she had out there on the grass

And I was quite flip in reply
that anyone who used plastic
had to expect things to skid

and break, that I couldn't worry
that her son might have been hurt
by whatever it was I sent skidding

down on them.

It was just then I went into my house
and to my utter astonishment
found my mother sitting there

as she always had sat, as must she always
forever sit there her head lolling
into sleep? Awake, awake my mother

what wind will lift you too
forever from the tawdriness,
make you rich as all those souls

crave crave crave

to be rich?

They are right. We must have
what we want. We cannot afford
not to. We have only one course:

the nets which entangle us are flames

                O souls, burn
                alive, burn now

                that you may forever
                have peace, have

                what you crave

                O souls,
                go into everything,
                let not one knot pass
                through your fingers

                let not any they tell you
                you must sleep as the net
                comes through your authentic hands

                What passes
                is what is, what shall be, what has
                been, what hell and heaven is
                is earth to be rent, to shoot you
                through the screen of flame which each knot
                hides as all knots are a wall ready
                to be shot open by you

                          the nets of being
                are only eternal if you sleep as your hands
                ought to be busy. Method, method

I too call on you to come
to the aid of all men, to women most
who know most, to woman to tell
men to awake. Awake, men,
awake

I ask my mother
to sleep. I ask her
to stay in the chair.
My chair
is in the corner of the fence.
She sits by the fireplace made of paving stones. The blue deer
need not trouble either of us.

And if she sits in happiness the souls
who trouble her and me
will also rest. The automobile

has been hauled away.

Variations Done for
Gerald Van De Wiele

I. Le Bonheur

dogwood flakes
what is green

the petals
from the apple
blow on the road

mourning doves
mark the sway
of the afternoon, bees
dig the plum blossoms

the morning
stands up straight, the night
is blue from the full of the April moon

iris and lilac, birds
birds, yellow flowers
white flowers, the Diesel
does not let up dragging
the plow

      as the whippoorwill,
the night's tractor, grinds
his song

      and no other birds but us
are as busy (O saisons, o chateaux!

Délires!

            What soul
is without fault?

Nobody studies
happiness

Every time the cock crows
I salute him

I have no longer any excuse
for envy. My life

has been given its orders: the seasons
seize

the soul and the body, and make mock
of any dispersed effort. The hour of death

is the only trespass

II. The Charge

dogwood flakes
the green

the petals from the apple-trees
fall for the feet to walk on

the birds are so many they are
loud, in the afternoon

they distract, as so many bees do
suddenly all over the place

With spring one knows today to see
that in the morning each thing

is separate but by noon
they have melted into each other

and by night only crazy things
like the full moon and the whippoorwill

and us, are busy. We are busy
if we can get by that whiskered bird,

that nightjar, and get across, the moon
is our conversation, she will say

what soul
isn't in default?

can you afford not to make
the magical study

which happiness is? do you hear
the cock when he crows? do you know the charge,

that you shall have no envy, that your life
has its orders, that the seasons

seize you too, that no body and soul are one
if they are not wrought

in this retort? that otherwise efforts
are efforts? And that the hour of your flight

will be the hour of your death?

III. Spring

The dogwood
lights up the day.

The April moon
flakes the night.

Birds, suddenly,
are a multitude

The flowers are ravined
by bees, the fruit blossoms

are thrown to the ground, the wind
the rain forces everything. Noise—

even the night is drummed
by whippoorwills, and we get

as busy, we plow, we move,
we break out, we love. The secret

which got lost neither hides
nor reveals itself, it shows forth

tokens. And we rush
to catch up. The body

whips the soul. In its great desire
it demands the elixir

In the roar of spring,
transmutations. Envy

drags herself off. The fault of the body and the soul
—that they are not one—

the matutinal cock clangs
and singleness: we salute you

season of no bungling

The Librarian

The landscape (the landscape!) again: Gloucester,
the shore one of me is (duplicates), and from which
(from offshore, I, Maximus) am removed, observe.

In this night I moved on the territory with combinations
(new mixtures) of old and known personages: the leader,
my father, in an old guise, here selling books and manuscripts.

My thought was, as I looked in the window of his shop,
there should be materials here for Maximus, when, then,
I saw he was the young musician has been there (been before me)

before. It turned out it wasn't a shop, it was a loft (wharf-
house) in which, as he walked me around, a year ago
came back (I had been there before, with my wife and son,

I didn't remember, he presented me insinuations via
himself and his girl) both of whom I had known for years.
But never in Gloucester. I had moved them in, to my country.

His previous appearance had been in my parents' bedroom where I
found him intimate with my former wife: this boy
was now the Librarian of Gloucester, Massachusetts!

> Black space,
> old fish-house.
> Motions
> of ghosts.
> I,
> dogging

his steps.
He
(not my father,
by name himself
with his face
twisted
at birth)
possessed of knowledge
pretentious
giving me
what in the instant
I knew better of.

But the somber
place, the flooring
crude like a wharf's
and a barn's
space

I was struck by the fact I was in Gloucester, and that my daughter
was there—that I would see her! She was over the Cut. I
hadn't even connected her with my being there, that she was

here. That she was there (in the Promised Land—the Cut!
But there was this business, of poets, that all my Jews
were in the fish-house too, that the Librarian had made a party

I was to read. They were. There were many of them, slumped
around. It was not for me. I was outside. It was the Fort.
The Fort was in East Gloucester—old Gorton's Wharf, where the Library

was. It was a region of coal houses, bins. In one a gang
was beating someone to death, in a corner of the labyrinth
of fences. I could see their arms and shoulders whacking

down. But not the victim. I got out of there. But cops
tailed me along the Fort beach toward the Tavern

> The places still
> half-dark, mud,
> coal dust.

> There is no light
> east
> of the Bridge

> Only on the headland
> toward the harbor
> from Cressy's

> have I seen it (once
> when my daughter ran
> out on a spit of sand

> isn't even there.) Where
> is Bristow? when does I-A
> get me home? I am caught

> in Gloucester. (What's buried
> behind Lufkin's
> Diner? Who is

> Frank Moore?

Moonset, Gloucester,
December 1, 1957, 1:58 AM

Goodbye red moon
In that color you set
west of the Cut I should imagine
forever Mother

After 47 years this month
a Monday at 9 AM
you set I rise I hope
a free thing as probably
what you more were Not
the suffering one you sold
sowed me on Rise
Mother from off me
God damn you God damn me my
misunderstanding of you

I can die now I just begun to live

The Song

more than the sennet of the solstice pipe,
lovely though a hautboy is, now that the season
is indoors

Now that we are driven
and all outdoors
is no good

and the season
nor the hautboy
cover the tune,

we talk, pell-mell.
And when, for a moment,
nothing is said,

in this season still (and so forth
And it is
indoors)

And small as the group. Then,
more than the sennet of the solstice pipe,
lovely though the piping is,

and the season
still is cold

The Distances

So the distances are Galatea

and one does fall in love and desires
mastery

old Zeus—young Augustus

Love knows no distance, no place

is that far away or heat changes
into signals, and control

old Zeus—young Augustus

Death is a loving matter, then, a horror

we cannot bide, and avoid
by greedy life

we think all living things are precious
—Pygmalions

a German inventor in Key West
who had a Cuban girl, and kept her, after her death
in his bed

after her family retrieved her
he stole the body again from the vault

Torso on torso in either direction,
young Augustus

out via nothing where messages
are

or in, down La Cluny's steps to the old man sitting
a god throned on torsoes,

        old Zeus

Sons go there hopefully as though there was a secret, the object
to undo distance?

                                  They huddle there, at the bottom
of the shaft, against one young bum

                or two loving cheeks,

        Augustus?

You can teach the young nothing

                all of them go away, Aphrodite
tricks it out,

        old Zeus—young Augustus

You have love, and no object

            or you have all pressed to your nose
which is too close,

        old Zeus hiding in your chin your young
        Galatea

the girl who makes you weep, and you keep the corpse live by all
your arts

        whose cheek do you stroke when you stroke the stone face
        of young Augustus, made for bed in a military camp,
        o Caesar?

O love who places all where each is, as they are, for every moment,
yield
         to this man
             that the impossible distance
be healed,

         that young Augustus
         and old Zeus
be enclosed

         "I wake you,
stone. Love this man."

Cross-Legged,
the Spider and the Web

with this body worship her
if necessary arrange
to sit before her parts
and if she object as she might
ask her for your sake to cover
her head but stare to blindness
better than the sun look until
you know look look keep looking until
you do know you do know

May 31, 1961

the lilac moon of the earth's backyard
which gives silence to the whole house
falls down
out of the sky
over the fence

                  poor planet
          now reduced
          to disuse

who looks so big
and alive
I am talking to you

          The shades
          on the windows
          of the Centers'
          place
          half down
          like nobody else's
          lets the glass lower halves
          make quiet mouths at you

lilac moon

          old backyard bloom

The Lamp

you can hurry the pictures toward you but
there is that point that the whole thing itself
may be a passage, and that your own ability
may be a factor in time, in fact that
only if there is a coincidence of yourself
& the universe is there then in fact
an event. Otherwise—and surely here the cinema
is large—the auditorium can be showing
all the time. But the question is
how you yourself are doing, if you in fact
are equal, in the sense that as a *like power*
you also are there when the lights
go on. This wld seem to be a
matter of creation, not simply
the obvious matter, creation
itself. Who in fact is any of us
to be there at all? That's what
swings the matter, also—
the beam hanging from

for Jack Clarke, October
14th 1964

As snow lies on the hill love's blackness lies
upon my blood and I steer perfectly the sled, tears streaming
from the speed and blinding me as I tear automobiles aside and throw them
away as though they were such toys
who seek to kill me and I go on
to the valley floor frozen to the river's
bank, and the river too frozen and across until I smash
into its further bank, the side the other side of the valley goes equally
the other way from, my heart fully darkened by death's arrival
                                           life's blackness
fallen into my blood as love has
                           fallen as snow
into the river's course before the cold froze her surface and we race
out on her in love's blackness to nothing,
which we came from, clothed now to fall like this faster than
all back into blood

the Heart is a clock
around which clusters
or which draws to itself
all which is the same
as itself in anything

or anyone else the
power of itself lies
all about itself in
a mathematic of feeling
which we call love

but who
love itself is the container
of all feelings otherwise than love
as well

as the Heart equally
holds all else there is anywhere
in Creation, when it is
full

II   [from *The Maximus Poems*]

Maximus, to himself

I have had to learn the simplest things
last. Which made for difficulties.
Even at sea I was slow, to get the hand out, or to cross
a wet deck.

        The sea was not, finally, my trade.
But even my trade, at it, I stood estranged
from that which was most familiar. Was delayed,
and not content with the man's argument
that such postponement
is now the nature of
obedience,

            that we are all late
            in a slow time,
            that we grow up many
            And the single
            is not easily
            known

It could be, though the sharpness (the *achiote*)
I note in others,
makes more sense
than my own distances. The agilities

            they show daily
            who do the world's
            businesses
            And who do nature's
            as I have no sense
            I have done either

I have made dialogues,
have discussed ancient texts,
have thrown what light I could, offered
what pleasures
doceat allows

But the known?
This, I have had to be given,
a life, love, and from one man
the world.
Tokens.
But sitting here
I look out as a wind
and water man, testing
And missing
some proof

I know the quarters
of the weather, where it comes from,
where it goes. But the stem of me,
this I took from their welcome,
or their rejection, of me

And my arrogance
was neither diminished
nor increased,
by the communication

2

It is undone business
I speak of, this morning,
with the sea
stretching out
from my feet

The Twist

Trolley-cars
are my inland waters
(Tatnuck Sq, and the walk
  from the end of the line
  to Paxton, for May-flowers

  or by the old road to Holden,
  after English walnuts

And my wife has a new baby
in a house at the end of
such a line, and the morning after,
is ready to come home, the baby too,
exceptionally well & advanced

Or he and I distinguish
between chanting,
and letting the song lie
in the thing itself.
I plant flowers
(xenia) for him,
in the wet soil, indoors,
in his house

As I had it in my first poem,
the Annisquam
fills itself, at its tides, as she did
the French dress, cut
on the bias,

              my neap,
my spring-tide, my
waters

1

Between Newton and Tatnuck Square the tracks
go up hill, the cars
sway, as they go around the bend
before they take, before they go down to
the outer-land
(where it is Sunday,
    I am small, people go off
    what strikes me as questionable
    directions. They are large,
    going away from my father and me,
    as cows on that landscape

    he and I seeming
    the only ones who know
    what we are doing, where
    we are going

Now I find out it is the Severn
goes from Worcester to Gloucester to
: Bristow, Smith called it,
what sticks in me as the promised land
those couples did go to, at right angles
from us, what does show
between Gloucester and Boston, the landscape

I go up-dilly, elevated, tenement
down

2

It rained,
the day we arrived.
And I have rowed the harbor since,
out the window of Johnny's Candy Kitchen,
through that glass and rain through which I looked
the first time I saw
the sea.

     She was staying,
after she left me,
in an apartment house
was like cake

     When I found her
—the people in it like Macomber
who lived under me on Charles St—next door
a man in a bowler hat scutted away,
the same man had fired a bullet
into her ho-ho

     Or it was Schwartz,
the bookie, whose mother-in-law
I'd have gladly gone to bed with

    Her room (the house
was a *dobostorte*), the door
high up on the wall,
48,

small,
like an oven-door

The harbor the same,
the night of the St Valentine
storm: the air
sea   ground   the same, tossed
ice   wind   snow   (Pytheus) one

                cakes falling
as quiet as I was
out of the sky as quiet
as the blizzard was

3

When I woke
in the toy house I had headed for, the look
out my window
sent me, the whiteness
in the morning sun, the figures
shoveling

        I went home
as fast as I could,

the whole Cut
was a paper village my Aunt Vandla
had given me, who gave me,
each Christmas,
such toys

As dreams are, when the day
encompasses. They tear down
the Third Ave El. Mine stays,
as Boston does, inches up.
I run my trains
on a monorail, I am seized
—not so many nights ago—
by the sight of the river
exactly there at the Bridge

where it goes out & in

I recognize
the country not discovera,
the marsh behind, the ditch that Blynman made, the dog-rocks
the tide roars over

      some curves off,
when it's the river's turn, shoots
calyx and corolla by the dog
                        (August,
the flowers break off

      but the anther,
the filament of now, the mass
drives on,

      the whole of it
coming,
to this pin-point
to turn

      in this day's sun,

in this veracity

there, the waters of several of them the roads

here, a blackberry blossom

a Plantation a beginning

I sit here on a Sunday
with grey water, the winter
staring me in the face

"the Snow lyes indeed
about a foot thicke
for ten weekes" John White

warns any prospective
planter

Fourteen spare men the first
year who huddled
above Half Moon beach

or got out of the onshore
breeze by clustering
what sort of what shacks

around the inshore harbor side
of Stage Head where now lovers
have a park and my mother

and my wife were curious
what went on in back seats
and Pat Foley

was furious some guy
on all four legs
crawled

about, to get a better view
when Pat sat spooning (where leisure
occupies shore

where fishing worke
was first set up, and fourteen men
did what with Gloucester's nothing land

and all her harbor?

The ship which brought them
we don't even know
its name, or Master

as they called a Capt
then, except that that
first season, 1623

the fishing, Gloucester
was good: the small ship (the *Fellowship?*) sailed
for Bilbao full

It cost the Company
200 pounds ($10,000)
to try these men

ashore that year,
to plant a land
was thinnest dust

to trade for furs
where smallpox
had made Champlain's

Indians of 1606
as thin as dogs
come in to hover

around what campfires
these fourteen Englishmen
managed

where I as young man berthed
a skiff and scarfed
my legs to get up rocks

this coast is all it's
made of, not soil
not beaver

fish fish fish

Her cargo brought
the Spanish market
exactly the same

the Company spent
Stage Fort: 200
pounds. Thus loss

that season. For the ship's
own charge
was more

for voyage; and her cost,
to buy her when they launched
the adventure

of the new frontier
(not boom, or gold,
the lucky strike,

but work, a fishing
"have set up",
said Smith, "this year

upon the Coast
about 50. English
ships

and by Cape Anne
Dorchester men
a plantation

a beginning") the ship alone
small fiftie tunnes
new sute of sayles amounted

to more than three hundred
pound. And now by Reason
the Voyage

was undertaken
too late, And the whole Provenue
was too little,

the deficit
It cost
$30,000

to get
Gloucester
started

Maximus, to Gloucester

I don't mean, just like that, to put down
the Widow Babson whose progeny and property
is still to be found and felt on Main
and Middle Streets, at Joppa, or
in Wellesley Hills (my Aunt Vandla
had a house on Laurel Avenue before
Babson had his Institute there and once,
when I was older, I swung by,
in a girl's father's Hupmobile
and lawd, how the house had been inflated
in my mem-o-ry

Or Jeffrey Parsons whom the historian Babson
clearly places over the Cut as the man who owned
all the land and boulders, all the hill and hollow
I know best in all the world, how Stage Fort is
what Babson called it, the only hundred acres
on this cape could possibly have fit the foolish hope
of Somerset and Dorset men to do on this rock coast
what England might have thought New England might be

But just there lies the thing, that "fisherman's Field"
(Stage Head, Stage Fort, and now and all my childhood
a down-dilly park for cops and robbers, baseball, firemen's
hose, North End Italian Sunday spreads, night-time Gloucester
monkey-business) stays the first place Englishmen
first felt the light and winds, the turning, from that view,
of what is now the City—the gulls the same but otherwise the sounds
were different for those fourteen men, probably the ocean

ate deeper in the shore, crashed further up at Cressy's (why
they took their shelter either side of softer Stage Head and let
Tablet Rock buff for them the weather side: on the lee,
below the ridge which runs from my house straight to Tablet Rock
these Dorset Somerset men built the Company house which Endicott
thought grand enough to pull it down and haul it all the way
to Salem for his Governor's abode:

> an house built at Cape Ann
> whc Walter Knight & the rest sd
> they built for Dorchester men

The point is not that Beverly
turned out to be their home,
that Conant Norman Allen Knight
Balch Palfrey Woodbury Tilly Gray
are Babsons Parsons there

> But that as I sit
> in a rented house
> on Fort Point,
> the Cape Ann Fisheries
>
> out one window,
> Stage Head looking me
> out of the other
> in my right eye
>
> (like backwards
> of a scene
> I saw the other way
> for thirty years)

          Gloucester can view
          those men
          who saw her
          first

He left him naked,
the man said, and
nakedness
is what one means

that all start up
to the eye and soul
as though it had never
happened before

          A year that year
          was new to men
          the place had bred
          in the mind of another

          John White had seen it
          in his eye
          but fourteen men
          of whom we know eleven

          twenty-two eyes
          and the snow flew
          where gulls now paper
          the skies

          where fishing continues
          and my heart lies

Some Good News

how small the news was
a permanent change had come
by 14 men setting down
on Cape Ann, on the westerly side
of the harbor

        the same side Bradford,
the fall before, had asked London
to get for him
so that New Plymouth
could prosecute fishing, no place,

in the minds of men, England
or on the ground, equal,
and fitting the future
as this Cape sitting
between the old

North Atlantic (of Biskay,
and Breton, of Cabot's
nosing into, for Bristol)
and the new—Georges
(as the bank was called as early

as 1530: who gave her their
patron saint—England?
Aragon? or Portyngales?)
Or Old Man's Pasture, Tillies
Bank, whichever way

you take what advantage
Cape Ann: Levett
says "too faire a gloss"
is placed on her,
the same year

New Plymouth here,
Dorchester there,
and Levett himself,
at Quack, care
to be right. 1623,

all of them,
suddenly,
pay attention,
to what fishermen
(since when? before
1500) have

been showing: the motion
(the Westward motion)
comes here,
to land. Stations
(going back to sheep,
and goats on Sable

Island, of all sand spits
upon the globe, and terror
of blown or dragged or dropped
earth in the midst of
water—shoals, worse

than rock because
they do blow shift lie,
are changing as you sound—
on this crooked sand
Portuguese (when?)

had a fishing station.
It wasn't new,
what happened,
at Cape Ann. It's where,
and when it

did. Smith
at Monhegan,
1614, and telling
about it, in a book,
1616, is

the demarcation (he,
the Sea-Marke!
as competently Columbus
backwards as Grant
forward, John Smith

the stater of
quantity and
precision, the double
doesn't unravel
so you'd know it

just like that, dragging,
as we do
shifty new

land, sucks
down, into the terrible

inert of
nature (the Divine
Inert, the literary man
of these men
of the West,

who knew private
passivity as these
quartermasters knew
supplies, said
it has to be

if princes
of the husting
are to issue from
the collapse
of the previous

soul: Smith,
too early yet
to be understood
to be the sign
of present

paternities—braggart
fisherman, the
Androgyne who hates
the simulacrum
Time Magazine

takes for male,
the playing coy
with identity)
a man's
struggle

with Caesar's
dream,
that he'd been intimate
with his mother,
and the soothsayer

eased him: it only means
that you shall conquer
the world. Smith,
as Sam Grant after,
was futile

until the place
and time burned
with the same heat as
the man (it isn't
for us to say

what a proper fire
is, it's what,
like Corinth
burning down
produces bronze—

or my Cabbage, we
baked potatoes
Fisher's Hill—or Caesar

dreamed, in Spain—or Smith,
who came to Monhegan

to catch whales,
and found cod, instead.
And furs. And Frenchmen
ahead of him, west
of him. Yet

Smith
changed
everything: he pointed
out
Cape Ann,

named her
so it's stuck,
and Englishmen,
who were the ones
who wanted to,

sat down, planted
fisheries
so they've stayed put,
on this coast, from Pemaquid
to Cape Cod.

One needs
grab hold of,
with purchase
this purpose, that
the Continental Shelf

was Europe's
first West, it wasn't
Spain's
south: fish,
and furs

and timber,
were wealth,
neither plants,
old agricultural
growing, from

Neolithic, sickles
& that kind of
contemplation
of nature, she
the brooder

nor gold, and murder.
We kill
as a fisherman's
knife nicks
abundance.

Which we take
for granted,
we don't even earn
our labor (as patriarchy
and matriarchy)

we do it all
by quantity and

machine. The subjective
hides, or runs riot
("vainglorious",

they put Smith down
as, and hire a Standish
to do corporative
murder: keep things clean,
by campaigns

drop bombs. One cries Mongols
instead. Yet Grant

still is a name
for butcher, for how
he did finally hammer out
a victory over

Clotho Lee, the spinner
the stocking frame
undid: textile
us, South
and North—the world,

tomorrow, and all
without fate
tomorrow,
if we,
who come from a housekeeping

which old mother Smith
started,
don't find out the inert

is as gleaming as,
and as fat as,

fish—so
we move: sd the
literary man, from hidden places
sprang
the killer's
instrument

who is also
the boatsteerer.
The "lily-iron",
they called the swordfish
harpoon when Gloucester

still chased
the blue-backed
thing on Browns (east
of Monhegan, north
of Georges

        West
and south Smith
put down the claim;
and wrote
her paper
and her name

"The which
is riches
will change

the world'' not knowing,
as we don't,

he'd hang up,
and be
a mark for all
who on this coast
do fall,

aloof aloof,
and come no near,
we cry. Or we'll over,
and you better
follow us who

from the hustings (''trash'',
industrial fish
are called which Gloucester
now catches, all that the bottom
of Georges,

the Channel, Middle Ground,
Browns, Pollock Rip
yields, anything
nature puts in the sea
comes up,

it is cornucopia
to see it
working up a sluggish
treadle,
from a ship's hold

to the truck
which takes it to the De-Hy
to be turned into catfood,
and fertilizer, for nature's
fields

Out of these waters
inland, it went. From then
—from Smith—some good news
better
get after

John Burke

John Burke did not rise
when Councilman Smith, nor had he signed
the complimentary scroll
handlettered
by Franklin E. Hamilton
of Public Works

Staring into the torsion
of his own face Burke
sat solid in
refusal (as,
in matters of the soul a private man
lives torn
by inspectio
and judicium, the judge
or mischievous woman
who make hob
of us) sweat, Burke
sweat, indubitably,
in his aloneness—or he'd not have said,
"I am no hypocrite"

Against the greased ways
of the city now (of the nation) this politician
himself a twisted animal
swelling of mouth, followed
by squirrels as pilot fish
himself a shark will not

tolerate
the suave / the insolence
of agreement

While he had to listen, Smith,
sticking it at him by that ease of charm
gets everyone to put up sodas
in Sterling Drug, have lunch
of halibut au gratin at
the Tavern, and they all run
with their hands (give up their eyes)
to be pleased by the
please Mr Smith tells fable, Soap
Esop of the present, of beast
a man turned into (Burke)

"Obsessed by fear," sd Piety
with face of fat,
"worried his life away" (I can see Burke,
worrying—who knows a thing or two,
has written on his mouth of a weasel much
munching, a few places Smith
will never get into, who likes
long legs) Burke sat there and heard this parabolist
(the business man is now the minister) go on

"worrying,
something frightful was going to happen
to him" (when surely,
by all the vetos
of his voting record Burke's
attention

on what was happening
to the city, that it was being ribboned,
dolled up like Smith himself) "the fear,"

sd the ponderous Harvard fullback,
"the object of his fear" (Burke's fear)
"never came. The fear itself" (o city's
whore) "like a beast in the jungle,
devoured him" (what a morsel,
Burkey) "and he was unable"
(here we have it—city hall)
"to make any constructive
move"—la

> that you shall sit
> and dwell until the judge
> or goddess of all mischief
> (she holds a city in her hair)
> directs you to your life

———————————

Steele then asked for a rising vote
to pass the resolutions inscribed
upon the councillor's scroll.

Every council member rose
except Burke, who remained in his chair,
staring at the table

A FOOTNOTE TO THE ABOVE,

> To speak in Yana-Hopi about these matters
> with which I, as Maximus, am concerned

(which is Gloucester, and myself as here-
a-bouts, in other words in *Maximus* local
relations are nominalized) one would talk,
Yana being a North California tongue, &
Hopi is a language peculiarly adjusted to
the topological as a prime and libidinal
character of a man, and therefore of all of his
proximities: metric then is mapping, and so,
to speak modern cant, congruent means of
making a statement), I, as Mr. Foster, went
to Gloucester, thus:

> "And past-I-go
> Gloucester-insides
> being Fosterwise of
> Charley-once-boy
> insides"

April Today Main Street

As against now the Gloucester
which came late enough, April, 1642, to stick

April today Main Street the sun
was warm enough I could stay

out of the mean easterly was coming up
each cross street

from the harbor, talked to the cop
at the head of Duncan, discovered that Joe,

the barber, had inherited the Fredericksons'
shop, that it was Mrs Galler, not the Weiners

"winers" the cigar woman and the greeting card
clerk in Sterling pronounced it

as I said her husband
they said he died

in front of her here
in the store

the street
was rife

of its hills,
and me going

with its
polyconic

character, the slipping
of Main

to Vinson's Cove,
now fill, and parking

with a baker, from Sao Paolo
where the spring

(I was surprised
to learn yesterday, that Eveleth

was a baker in Boston
in 1642, before he came and possessed

so much of Meeting House
Green) The Gloucester which held

was three power points,
three nexuses

and the General Court:
what Endecott

and Downing
divided, April that year

how a town
was created

2 mo 42
There was a stage

on Duncan's Point,
the formulary

for patent or joint
stock company stating

it was Mr Thomson's,
London merchant,

one man mentioned,
the other backers

not named, instead, intend
the Court goes on

to promote
the fishing

trade, trying to turn
Massachusetts into

the staple intended
said Smith, the Indies

lying just
offshore to be drawn up

on silk lines & glowing hooks
fishermen in palanquins, robed women

watching, holding children
on the shore, a daisy world, the silver ore

codfish. "It was ordered"
(the Company

of the Massachusetts ,
Bay) "that a fishing

be begun, that the said
Mr Thomson, and other necessaries

for that use, shall have sufficient lands allowed,
like railroad companies: how little,

until England
was cut off

by her own trouble (that the Scotch border
had been crossed December

1640 Winthrop
learned from that post office

of the North Atlantic, Smith's
Isles

of Shoals
within weeks) did any of them

know what it would mean
to have these mines

in their waters
to go to

to sell
to Fayal

to go to St Kitts
to take away Newfoundland

to make Spain, and Turks,
to start to make any ocean

a Yankee lake, this fellow here
named Osmund Dutch (or was William

Southmead also) but definitely
Thomas Millward (who went to

Newbury) ''Slow'',
Smith cried,

upon you
as he died

There is evidence
a frame

of Mr Thomson's
did

exist, Will Southmead's
ux, alia Ash, did sell

to John Jackson, John Jackson
to Peter Duncan, but I write in

the first letter (after Conant's two)
to go

home,
to England: ''Me Osmundū Douch

De Capae Annae
in nova Anglia, nautā

Dat' 18.5.1639
presented himself and said

take this letter
to my wife

                    Grace,

my love

remembered
to you

in the Lord, These
are to lett you understand

that God be praysed I am
in health heere

in this Country
and so I hope

are you together
with our Children. Seeing it hath pleased God

to bless me heere I have cleared
40£ and shall be able

for to entertaine you
to make good provision

come over
taking such care

as to bring .   .   . Mr. Millward
my partner, of Noddles Island

in the fishing trade
which we now are setting on"   1641: Abraham Robinson

Thomas Ashley Willm
Browne

rent a sloop
of 3 tunes, are to pay

3£ in good and merchantable
dry fish in 3 months

—a Biskie shallop?
to go with Biskie Island?

to this hour sitting
as the mainland hinge

of the 128 bridge
now brings in

what,
to Main Street?

MAXIMUS, FROM DOGTOWN—I

The sea was born of the earth without sweet union of love Hesiod says

But that then she lay for heaven and she bare the thing which encloses
every thing, Okeanos the one which all things are and by which nothing
is anything but itself, measured so

screwing earth, in whom love lies which unnerves the limbs and by its
heat floods the mind and all gods and men into further nature

                                Vast earth rejoices,

deep-swirling Okeanos steers all things through all things,
everything issues from the one, the soul is led from drunkenness
to dryness, the sleeper lights up from the dead,
the man awake lights up from the sleeping

    WATERED ROCK
of pasture meadow orchard road where Merry
died in pieces tossed by the bull he raised himself to fight
in front of people, to show off his
                    Handsome Sailor ism

died as torso head & limbs
in a Saturday night's darkness
drunk trying
to get the young bull down
to see if Sunday morning again he might

before the people show off
once more
his prowess—braggart man to die
among Dogtown meadow rocks

                              "under" the dish
                              of the earth
                              Okeanos under
                              Dogtown
                              through which (inside of which) the sun passes
                              at night—
                                        she passes the sun back to
                              the east through her body
                              the Geb (of heaven) at night

              Nut is water
              above & below, vault
              above and below
              watered rock on which
              by which Merry
              was so many pieces
              Sunday morning

subterranean and celestial
primordial water holds
Dogtown high
                    And down
the ice holds
Dogtown, scattered
boulders little bull
who killed

Merry
            who sought to manifest
his soul, the stars
manifest their souls

                    my soft sow the roads
of Dogtown trickling like from underground rock
springs under an early cold March moon

                                        or hot summer and my son
                                        we come around a corner
                                        where a rill
                                        makes Gee Avenue in a thin
                                        ford

                                            after we see a black duck
                                        walking across a populated
                                        corner

                                                life spills out

Soft soft rock
Merry died by
in the black night

fishermen lived
in Dogtown and came
when it was old to whore
on Saturday nights
at three girls' houses

Pisces eternally swimming
inside her overhead
their boots or the horse

clashing the sedimentary
rock tortoise shell
she sits on the maternal beast
of the moon and the earth

Not one mystery
nor man
possibly not even a bird
heard Merry
fight that bull by
(was Jeremiah Millett's house

Drunk
to cover his shame,
blushing Merry
in the bar
walking up

to Dogtown to try
his strength,
the baby bull
now full grown

waiting,
not even knowing
death
was in his power over
this man who lay
in the Sunday morning sun
like smoked fish
in the same field

fly-blown and a colony
of self-hugging grubs—handsome
in the sun, the mass
of the dead and the odor
eaten out of the air
by the grubs sticking
moving by each other
as close as sloths

> she is the goddess
> of the earth, and night
> of the earth and fish
> of the little bull
> and of Merry

> > Merry
> > had a wife

> She is the heavenly mother
> the stars are the fish swimming
> in the heavenly ocean she has
> four hundred breasts

> Merry could have used
> as many could have drunk
> the strength he claimed
> he had, the bravo

> Pulque in Spain
> where he saw the fight
> octli in Mexico
> where he wanted to

show off
dead in Gloucester
where he did

The four hundred gods
of drink alone
sat with him
as he died
in pieces

In 400 pieces
his brain shot
the last time the bull
hit him pegged him
to the rock

     before he tore him
to pieces

     the night sky
looked down

Dogtown is soft
in every season
high up on her granite
horst, light growth
of all trees and bushes
strong like a puddle's ice
the bios
of nature in this
park of eternal
events is a sidewalk

to slide on, this
terminal moraine:

the rocks the glacier tossed
toys
Merry played by
with his bull

       400 sons of her only
       would sit
       by the game

       All else was in the sky
       or in town
       or shrinking solid rock

       We drink
       or break open
       our veins solely
       to know. A drunkard
       showing himself in public
       is punished
       by death

       The deadly power of her
       was there that night
       Merry was born
       under the pulque-sign

       The plants of heaven
       the animals of the soul
       were denied

Joking men
had laughed
at Merry

Drink
had made him
brave

Only the sun
in the morning
covered him
with flies

Then only
after the grubs
had done him
did the earth
let her robe
uncover and her part
take him in

Maximus to Gloucester, Letter 27 [withheld]

I come back to the geography of it,
the land falling off to the left
where my father shot his scabby golf
and the rest of us played baseball
into the summer darkness until no flies
could be seen and we came home
to our various piazzas where the women
buzzed

To the left the land fell to the city,
to the right, it fell to the sea

I was so young my first memory
is of a tent spread to feed lobsters
to Rexall conventioneers, and my father,
a man for kicks, came out of the tent roaring
with a bread-knife in his teeth to take care of
a druggist they'd told him had made a pass at
my mother, she laughing, so sure, as round
as her face, Hines pink and apple,
under one of those frame hats women then

This, is no bare incoming
of novel abstract form, this

is no welter or the forms
of those events, this,

Greeks, is the stopping
of the battle

It is the imposing
of all those antecedent predecessions, the precessions

of me, the generation of those facts
which are my words, it is coming

from all that I no longer am, yet am,
the slow westward motion of

more than I am

There is no strict personal order

for my inheritance.

        No Greek will be able

to discriminate my body.

        An American

is a complex of occasions,

themselves a geometry

of spatial nature.

        I have this sense,

that I am one

with my skin

        Plus this—plus this:

that forever the geography

which leans in

on me I compell

backwards I compell Gloucester

to yield, to

change

        Polis

is this

Maximus Letter # whatever

chockablock

Once a man was traveling through the woods, and
he heard some distance off a sound of feet beat-
ing the ground. He went to find the people who
made the sound, and it was a full week before
he came to them. It was a man and his wife danc-
ing around a tree in the top of which was a rac-
coon. By their constant treading they had worn
a trench in the ground, and were in it up to their
waists. When the man asked them why they did it
they said they were hungry and they were trying
to dance the tree down to catch the raccoon.

Now the man told them there was a better way to
fell a tree, a new way, and he showed them how to
cut it down. In return for which he asked the skin
if they had the meat of the raccoon. So they tanned
it and off he went.

Another distance, in the path in the forest, he
met another man who was carrying his house on his
head. He was frightened at first but the man put
his house down and shook hands with him, and while
they had a smoke together, and talked, the man
noticed the raccoon skin and asked where he got
it. He told him, from the dancing man and his wife.

This was enough to get the other started. He offered
him anything for the skin and finally the house. Look-

ing it over our man was delighted to find it had so
many rooms and such good furniture. But he said I
never could carry it as you do. Yes, sd the man who
belonged somewhere else, just try it, and he found he
could, it was as light as a basket.

So he went off carrying his house until night when
he came to a hard-wood ridge near a good spring of
water and put it down. Inside was a wide bed covered
with a white bear-skin, and it was very soft, and he
was tired and he slept very well. In the morning, it
was even better. Hanging from the beams were deer-
meat, hams, duck, baskets of berries and maple sugar,
and as he reached out for them the rug itself melted
and it was white snow, and his arms turned into wings
and he flew up to the food and it was birch-boughs on
which it hung, and he was a partridge and it was spring.

Maximus, at the Harbor

Okeanos rages, tears rocks back in his path.

Encircling Okeanos tears upon the earth to get love loose,

that women fall into the clefts

of women, that men tear at their legs

and rape until love sifts

through all things and nothing is except love as stud

upon the earth

love to sit in the ring

of Okeanos love to lie in the spit

of a woman a man to sit in her legs

(her hemispheres

loomed above me,

I went to work

like the horns of a snail

Paradise is a person. Come into this world.

The soul is a magnificent Angel.

And the thought of its thought is the rage

of Ocean   :   apophainesthai

roared the great bone on to Norman's

Woe; apophainesthai, as it blew

up a pool on Round Rock shoal;

apophainesthai it cracked as it broke

on Pavilion Beach; apophainesthai

it tore at Watch House Point

        II

           apophainesthai
           got hidden all the years
           apophainesthai: the soul,
           in its progressive rise

           apophainesthai
           passes in & out
           of more difficult things
           and by so passing
           apophainesthai

           the act which actuates the soul itself—
           she loomed before me and he stood
           in this room—it sends out
           on the path ahead the Angel
           it will meet

                apophainesthai

           its ascent is its own mirage

III

The great Ocean is angry. It wants the Perfect Child

October 23rd and 4th
1961

A Later Note on
Letter # 15

In English the poetics became meubles—furniture—
thereafter (after 1630

& Descartes was the value

until Whitehead, who cleared out the gunk
by getting the universe in (as against man alone

& that concept of history (not Herodotus's,
which was a verb, to find out for yourself:
'istorin, which makes any one's acts a finding out for him or her
self, in other words restores the traum: that we act somewhere

at least by seizure, that the objective (example Thucidides, or
the latest finest tape-recorder, or any form of record on the spot

—live television or what—is a lie

as against what we know went on, the dream: the dream being
self-action with Whitehead's important corollary: that no event

is not penetrated, in intersection or collision with, an eternal
event

The poetics of such a situation
are yet to be found out

January 15, 1962

155

CHRONICLES

1

As Zeus sent Hermes
to draw Agenor's cattle
down to the seashore
at Tyre, date

1540 BC, and thereby
caused the pursuit
of him by Agenor's
sons—one to

Carthage, one to the edge
of the Black Sea, one
to found Thebes,
another

to establish the rich
gold mines of Thasos—
meanwhile Zeus
as an immaculate

white bull with one
black stripe down him
has caught Europe
up on to his back,

his softness
fooling her,
she placing flowers
in his mouth,

he sails off
to Crete, near
Ida, and there
also Phoenician

persons are
born, Europe's
sons Minos,
Rhadamanthys,
Sarpedon

2

Taurus,
King of Crete,
caught Tyre
when Agenor

and his sons
were rallying
from a sea-
battle,

and plastered
it—the Evil Night
of Tyre John Malalas
calls it,

when Cretans
took everything
and blasted her
back in to the sea

from which
she came, when
Ousoos the
hunter

was the first man
to carve out
the trunk
of a tree

and go out
on the waters
from the shore

These
are the chronicles
of an imaginary
town

placed as an island
close to the shore

THE GULF OF MAINE

Altham says
they were in a pinnace
off Monhegan
season
1623, having left
Cape Anne

and trove
mightily
until in
Damariscove Harbor they
split up
in a storm

the sides
of the vessel
with the current running North North East
were ground
in turn
by the same rock wall the vessel

switching about
like a bob and his wife
and Captain Bridge's, in London
reached by mail via
Plymouth's agent

address
High Court Row and St by Chancery Light
could not have imagined
had they known,

that night,
their husbands

were on such a shore
and bandied
as they were: 4 men
alone, of all of them,

dragged themselves up
in the early morn
out of the wash
of that dreadful storm
so many chips among ground timbers

of what was left
of the pinnace. Such was the coast
when sturdy oak-built 17th-century
little boats out of London and Plymouth
cast their nets, King James said We do approve

of the Pilgrimes going
to the sand shore of
Virginiay
if fishing is
the holy calling

they go there
about, dear James for corfish
did they go Madame Altham
Madame Bridge
called on James Shirley

one bright City morning
for pounds and sterling
sturdy pence
in recompense
of their dear husbands

so. The night
was growley
the waves
were high the high built pinnas
tossed the winds down
pressed

the Little James
until she was far spent
& fore went head down
into the sea below the
waves her sticky masts

with thick crows nests
were up above the
waves and broken-stumped
wild balls of fire
played over

where their heads
below the water
filled and shoes
and coats pulled down
the crew

and Captain Bridge
& Mr Altham swam
like underbodies going by
in an outrageous park

or film until
their knees
were smashed
on small rocks
as their poor pinnace likewise poorly lay

chawn mostly but some parts of her bruised sides
now resting on the sands where we shall
dig them up and set them upright as posts
at just the signal place for tourists
to come by and not give one idea

why such odd culls
stand along a fishing
shore
though not used much at the present time
and mostly well-dressed persons
frequent it

And now let all the ships come in

pity and love the Return the Flower

the Gift and the Alligator catches

—and the mind go forth to the end of the world

"at the boundary of the mighty world" H. (T) 620 foll.

Now Called Gravel Hill—dogs eat
gravel

Gravelly hill was 'the source and end (or boundary' of
D'town on the way that leads from the town to Smallmans
now Dwelling house, the Lower
Road gravelly, how the hill was, not the modern usableness
of any thing but leaving it as an adverb as though the Earth herself
was active, she had her own characteristics, she could
stick her head up out of the earth at a spot
and say, to Athena I'm stuck here, all I can show
is my head but please, do something about
this person I am putting up out of the ground into your hands

Gravelly hill 'father' Pelops otherwise known as
Mud Face founder of
Dogtown. That sort of 'reason': leave things alone.
As it is there isn't a single thing isn't an opportunity
for some 'alert' person, including practically everybody
by the 'greed', that, they are 'alive', therefore. Etc.
That, in fact, there are 'conditions'. Gravelly Hill
or any sort of situation for improvement, when
the Earth was properly regarded as a 'garden
tenement messuage orchard and if this is nostalgia
let you take a breath of April showers
let's us reason how is the dampness in your

nasal passage—but I have had lunch
in this 'pasture' (B. Ellery to
                    George Girdler Smith
                        'gentleman'
                          1799, for
                          £ 150)

overlooking
'the town'
sitting there like
the Memphite lord of
all Creation

with my back—with Dogtown
over the Crown of
gravelly
hill

It is not bad
to be pissed off

where there is *any*
condition imposed, by whomever, no matter how close

any
quid pro quo
get out. Gravelly Hill says
leave me be, I am contingent, the end of the world
is the borders
of my being

I can even tell you
where I run out; and you can find
out. I lie here
so many feet up
from the end of an old creek
which used to run off
the Otter ponds. There is a bridge
of old heavy slab stones
still crossing the creek on
the 'Back Road' about three rods
from where I do end northerly, and from my Crown
you may observe, in fact Jeremiah Millett's
generous pasture
which, in fact, is the first 'house'
(of Dogtown) is a part of the slide of
my back, to the East: it isn't so decisive
how one thing does end
and another begin to be very obviously dull about it
I should like to take the time to be dull
there is obviously very much to be done and the fire depart-
    ment
rushed up here one day—they called it
Bull Field, in the newspaper—when just that
side of me I am talking about,
which belonged to Jeremiah Millett
and rises up rather sharply
—it became Mr Pulsifer's and then,
1799, the property of the town
of Gloucester—was burned off.
My point is, the end of myself,
happens, on the east side (Erechthonios)

to be the beginning of another set
of circumstance. The road,
which has gone around me, swings
just beyond where Jeremiah Millett had his house
and there's a big rock about ends my being,
properly, swings
to the northeast, and makes its way
generally staying northeast in direction
to Dogtown Square or the rear of
William Smallman's
house where rocks pile up
darkness,
in a cleft in the earth
made of a perfect pavement
                    Dogtown Square
of rocks alone March, the holy month
                    (the holy month,
                    LXIII
of nothing but black granite turned
every piece,
downward,
to darkness,
to chill
and darkness. From which the height above it even
in such a fearful congery
with a dominant rock like a small mountain
above the Hellmouth the back of Smallmans is
that this source and end of the way from the town into
the woods is only—as I am the beginning, and Gaia's
child—*katavóthra*. Here you enter

darkness. Far away from me, to the northeast,
and higher than I, you enter
the Mount,
which looks merry,
and you go up into it
feels the very same as the corner
where the rocks all are
even smoking a cigarette on the mount
nothing around you, not even the sky
relieves the pressure of this declivity
which is so rich and packed.
It is Hell's mouth
where Dogtown ends
(on the lower
of the two roads into
the woods.
I am the beginning
on this side
nearest the town
and it—this paved hole in the earth
is the end (boundary
Disappear.

I looked up and saw
its form
through everything
—it is sewn
in all parts, under
and over

having descried the nation
to write a Republic
in gloom on Watch-House Point

Main Street
is deserted, the hills
are bull-dozed
away.   The River alone,
and Stage Fort Park
where the Merrimac
once emptied under the ice
to the Banks survive

And on the Polls
at the edge

where the rocks are soft
from the scales

and in the heat-edges
grass and thorny

bushes
are   I idle

overlooking
                    creation

more versant
on the western side

than on the eastern

and several of these areas
on Dogtown Commons

than on the minds
of men, during the period

in which this district
was inhabited, brought into the state

of tilled fields and now appear
as small pasture lands devoid

of boulders. Humps
        of Devil's glens
on Great Hill, and just
at Dogtown Square
to strip the soul
into its wild
admissions

and one sit
in the starkness
as though this
were anything
and go away
left with one's own
resort, wishing
for grass and the air
of heaven.   Finding out
there is no doorstep
equal to the heart

of God   sitting by
the cellar
of Widow Day's
kame   These high-lying benches
of drift material
where subglacial streams emerged
lay down there fields when Dogtown lay
below the level of the sea, Fled

the softness
for the west

or the top of the hill, fled
the deserted streets   a December
                    stayed at home

until human beings came back,
until human beings

were the streets of the soul
love was in their wrinkles

they filled the earth, the positiveness
was in their being, they listened

to the sententious,
with ears of the coil of the sea

they were the paths of water green and rich
under the ice, carrying the stratified drift kame

dropping their self-hooded anger
into the dialogue of their beloveds
taking their own way to the throne of creation

the diorite
is included in the granitite

the granitite has burst up around
the diorite,
leaving it as an undivided mass

the power in the air
is prana

it is not seen
In the ice,

on top of the Poles,
on the throne

of the diorite, the air alone
is what I sit in

among the edges
of the plagioclase

Imbued
with the light

the flower
grows down

the air
of heaven

West Gloucester

Condylura
cristata
on Atlantic
Street West
Gloucester
spinning on its
star-wheel
nose,
in the middle of the
tarvia,

probably because it had been
knocked in the head (was
actually fighting all the time,
with its fore-paws at
the lovely mushroom growth
of its nose, snow-ball flake pink flesh
of a gentian, until I
took an oar out of the back seat of the station wagon
and removed it
like a pea on a knife to
the side of the road

stopped its dance dizzy dance
on its own nose out of its head
working as though it would get rid of
its own pink appendage

like a flower dizzy
with its own self

like the prettiest thing in the world drilling
itself into the

pavement

  and I gave it, I hope, all the marshes of Walker's Creek
to get it off what might also seem
what was wrong with it, that the highway
had magnetized the poor thing

the loveliest animal I believe I ever did see
in such a quandary

  and off the marshes
  of Walker's Creek fall
  graduatedly so softly to
  the Creek and the Creek to
  Ipswich Bay an arm
  of the Atlantic Ocean

  send the Star Nosed Mole
  all into the grass
  all away from the dizzying
  highway if that was what was wrong

  with the little thing, spinning
  in the middle of the
  highway

Stevens song

out of the fire out of the mouth
of his Father
eating him

Stevens ran off,

having called Charles the Second

a king he could not give allegiance to

Stevens was then

63 years old and did he ever

return?   when was the chief shipbuilder

of England and

the maritime world of the day (1683?)
in Gloucester, first doing
running off, where?
So that his wife had to petition
the General Court for relief
from his punishment for refusing
to sign the Oath of Allegiance

and his remarks
to officers of the Crown

which were considered
seditious (as my own Father's

remarks to Paddy Hehir
and to Blocky Sheehan

were considered
insubordinate

    that hemp you promised
    for caulking the pinnace

Stevens ran off
My father

stayed
& was ground down

to death, taking night collections
joining Swedish fraternal

organizations, seeking to fight back
with usual American political

means, Senator David I. Walsh, Congressman
Hobbs, Pehr Holmes Mayor and so forth

On the side
of the King the Father

there sits a wolf
which is not his own will

which comes from outside
it is not true

that the demon
is a poison in the blood

only, he is also
a principle

in creation, and enters unknown
to the being, he is different

it is true,
from the angel   but only

because he travels even further
to get inside, and is not bearing

light or color, or fruits, not one garden
ever a garden ever a walled place

not anything resembling Paradise

nor Sneferus'
intended ship

imported forty shiploads of cedar logs
from Byblos

and in 1954 AD,
when the funerary boat

of Kheops,
Sneferus' successor

happened to turn up
as previously undiscovered

in a shaft of the burial base
of the sd Kheops' pyramid

the boat,
which was intact,

gave off
the original odor

of its cedar wood fittings.   This also
is a possibility of the other

of the three matters here
under concern, of three kinds of way

by which the prince
is instructed

to have in his mouth
the ability to lend

aid
to the bewildered

mob.   the
creature, from outer space

who comes in unknown
and lives unknown

in the son, craving
to be able

to be himself, not the question
of youth not the matter

is he a male
is he a daughter even

or the daughter's
original question

either of them,
and not even in face of

the father or the mother, not any of that
the dirty filthy whining ultimate thing

entered,
when none present knew

entered as the dog,
slept in the night

tore the bloody cloak then
literally tore the flesh

of the conjoined
love I was

a dog who had
bitten into

her body
as it was joined

to mine,
naturally,

in normal bedstead
fashion, no excessive

facts here, no special
or sought meaning

no more than
that

the demon
the canine

head piercing
right through the letter carrier

trousers and into the
bone, the teeth of Fenris

craves and locks
directly

into
the flesh, there isn't

any room
except for

pieces, holes
are left

when
I was

a dog   when Tyr
put his hand

in Fenris
mouth

—it was not a test,
it was to end

that matter, Fenris
simply bit it

off Thereby
there awaits

a Reason: the Quest
is a Reason

          Stevens
went away across Cut Bridge

my father
lost his

life the son
of the King of the Sea walked

away from the filthy wolf
eating the dropped body, the

scavenger

Maximus to himself June
1964

> no more,
> where the tidal river rushes
>
> no more
> the golden cloak (beloved
> World)
>
> no more dogs
> to tear anything
> apart—the fabric
>
> nothing like
> the boat (no more Vessel
> in the Virgin's
> arms
>
> no more dog-rocks
> for the tide
> to rush over not any time again
> for wonder
>
> the ownership
> solely
> mine

COLE'S ISLAND

I met Death—he was a sportsman—on Cole's
Island. He was a property-owner. Or maybe
Cole's Island, was his. I don't know. The
point was I was there, walking, and—as it
often is, in the woods—a stranger, suddenly
showing up, makes the very thing you were do-
ing no longer the same. That is suddenly
what you thought, when you were alone, and
doing what you were doing, changes because someone else
shows up. He didn't bother me, or say anything. Which is
not surprising, a person might not, in the circumstances;
or at most a nod or something. Or they would. But they wouldn't,
or you wouldn't think to either, if it was Death. And
He certainly was, the moment I saw him. There wasn't any question
about that even though he may have looked like a sort of country
gentleman, going about his own land. Not quite. Not it being He.

A fowler, maybe—as though he was used to
hunting birds, and was out, this morning, keeping
his hand in, so to speak, moving around, noticing
what game were about. And how they seemed. And how the woods
were. As a matter of fact just before he had shown up,
so naturally, and as another person might walk
up on a scene of your own, I had noticed
a cock and hen pheasant cross easily the
road I was on and had tried, in fact,
to catch my son's attention quick enough for him

to see before they did walk off into the bayberry
or arbor vitae along the road.

My impression is we did—
that is, Death and myself, regard each other. And
there wasn't anything more than that, only that he had appeared,
and we did recognize each other—or I did, him, and he seemed
to have no question
about my presence there, even though I was uncomfortable.
  That is,
Cole's Island
is a queer isolated and gated place, and I was only there by will
to know more of the topography of it lying as it does out
over the Essex River. And as it now is, with no tenants that one can speak of,
it's more private than almost any place one might imagine.
And down in that part of it where I did meet him (about half way between the
two houses over the river and the carriage house
at the entrance) it was as quiet and as much a piece
of the earth as any place can be. But my difficulty,
when he did show up, was immediately at least that I was
an intruder, by being there at all
and yet, even if he seemed altogether
used to Cole's Island, and, like I say, as though he owned it,
even if I was sure he didn't, I noticed him, and he me, and he
went on without anything extraordinary at all.

Maybe he had gaiters on, or almost
a walking stick, in other words much more
habited than I,
who was in chinos actually and

only doing what I had set myself to do here
& in other places on Cape Ann.

It was his eye perhaps which makes me
render him as Death? It isn't true, there wasn't anything
that different about his eye,

it was not one thing more than that he was Death instantly
that he came into sight. Or that I was aware there was a person
here as well as myself. And son.

We did exchange some glance. That is the fullest possible
account I can give, of the encounter.

Wednesday, September 9th, 1964

Maximus, in Gloucester Sunday, LXV

Osmund Dutch, and John Gallop, mariners, their wages

asked that they be paid to the Dorchester

Co., July, 1632.   Thus Reverend John White writing

to John Winthrop at Boston locates

Dutch and Gallop as on this coast or ferrying

others across the Atlantic at a probable date earlier

than 1630.   With Abraham Robinson the two

then constitute the probable earliest

new coast types to follow

the original Stage Fort few, who were already

by the date 1630 or before

well hidden now by Beverly

marshes, and the farming creeks

of Bass River, exception

John Tilley who, like Gallop

shows on the life of the coast years

1628 thereafter coastal 'captains'

or Masters—'mariners so useful

valuable or innovators Banks

Coves —Slews are named still

after them

　　　　　　Now date August 1965 returning

Gloucester from as far out in the world as my own

wages draw me, and bitter

police cars turn my corner, no one in the world

close to me, alone in my home where a plantation

had been a Sunday earlier than this been

proposed, it is Osman (or Osmund) Dutch's

name, and Gallop whom I am closest to,

it turns out, once more drawn into the

plague of my own unsatisfying possible identity as

denominable Charles Olson add here as 4's

on a weather shingle our

names

　　　　　　Charles Olson

　　　　　　Osmund Dutch

　　　　　　John Gallop

　　　　　　Abraham Robinson, our

　　　　　　names (written 28

　　　　Stage Fort Avenue Gloucester

　　　　August 22nd 1965

Swimming through the air, in schools upon the highways,
                                          their minds
swimming in schools, the lower atmosphere
gelatinizing from their traffic, cities like cigarettes,
                                          country side
sacrificed to their eating time & space up like fish
Fish-people   their own UFOs   the end of Pisces
could be the end of species   Nature herself
left to each flying object passing in a mucus
surrounding the earth

Maximus of Gloucester

Only my written word

I've sacrificed every thing, including sex and woman
—or lost them—to this attempt to acquire complete
concentration. (The con-
ventual.) "robe and bread"
not worry or have to worry about
either

Half Moon beach ("the arms of her")
my balls rich as Buddha's
sitting in her like the Padma
—and Gloucester, foreshortened
in front of me. It is not I,
even if the life appeared
biographical. The only interesting thing
is if one can be
an image
of man, "The nobleness, and the arete."

(Later: myself (like my father, in the picture) a shadow
                on the rock.

Friday November 5th
1965

I have been an ability—a machine—up to
now. An act of "history", my own, and my father's,
together, a queer [Gloucester-sense] combination
of completing something both visionary—or illusions (projection? literally
lantern-slides, on the sheet, in the front-room Worcester,
on the wall, and the lantern always getting too hot
and I burning my fingers—& burning my
nerves   as in fact John says or Vincent Ferrini they too
had to deal with their father's existence.   My own
was so loaded in his favor as in fact so patently
against my mother that I have been like his stained shingle
ever since   Or once   or forever   It doesn't matter   The love I learned
from my father has stood me in good stead
—home stead—I maintained this "strand" to
this very day.   My father's   And now my own

                          I face
the snowy hills
of Stage Fort Park—hanging ground
And the hill behind
where Ben Kerr's house alone is still
stone
and the fore-hill
in front of my eye
(over Half Moon and between
Tablet Rock quite sharply marked
in mass
by the snow too [right up Kerr's hill skinny trees alone

declare,
with the snow,
the hill
     , the snow
on Half Moon ''hill,''
and Tablet Rock—''Washing rock,'' of the Parsonses?
and Stage Point their stage therefore Tablet
their washing Rock?
               my beach only
in <u>symbolic</u> fact   like wearing rubber suit
and going diving walking off heavily laden
like the Great Auk wobbling with lead all
weighing one at the waist
into the sea   I never
liked Half Moon beach   I liked Tablet Rock
and Cressys as I suppose my father also
he turned
         as I tend to too to the
         right when we
         left the house he walked and I
         grew up to meet him or stride after him
         when he had set off
         with his water-color box to paint
         a scene   Or
         as so often to
         go to the Coast Guard
         Station at
         Dollivers Neck   or moonlight nights the lengths
         of Hesperus Avenue to Rafe's Chasm (after
         when he was dead and I was young I'd

do likewise with a girl or
friends
       the T the shore
today pure
snow and "drawn"
in trees and shaped
in snow's
solidifying
rocks let stayed black
(as the tide,
withdrawn an hour say now from high
has this eye-view line Lane so also
used to show distances
back of each other   my father
And I
on the same land   like Pilgrims
come to shore
          he paid
          with his life dear Love to take me
          to Plymouth
        for their
        tercentenary
    there
the U.S. Post Office
using
his purpose to
catch him
in their trap   to bust him
organizing
Postal Workers

benefits—Retirement age
Widows pensions   a different
leadership in Washington than
Doherty   my father a Swedish
wave of
migration after
Irish? like Negroes
now like Leroy and Malcolm
X the final wave
of wash upon this
desperate
ugly
cruel
Land this Nation
which never
lets anyone
come to
shore: Cagli said
sitting on the grass of the baseball diamond
of the Industrial League and as Cut Eagles over
out of my sight
    at the moment
    behind Tablet Rock mass and
    Half Moon
    my Wop
    sayeth
  whom my Father
  in a dream said
  Ad Valorem
  Cagli Cagli said no one can sit

any length of time happily
or at comfort or rest
or by Seine's bank or
the eye rest coming from Da Vinci Airport
into Rome by bus last summer on those
utterly Etruscan
or Mesopotamian or Egyptian
Memphis-time
crazy
Houses of Solid Hay constructed
like permanent
Acropolises NOT STAGE FORT PARK not America not this land

                                        not this Nation
                                        short-winded

              the very Earth,
              here

And my Father
dead of the fight
he got caught by then into
by the time I was 24—15 years
from the date he took me
to Plymouth, the week
we stayed with Mr Brown the Postmaster
of North Plymouth
—Leroy's father a postmaster
in some small New Jersey place (just outside Newark? or substation of
                              that city Obadiah Bruen
1st Town Clerk of Gloucester
went on [from New London] to from after
having come to Gloucester from

Strawberry Bank? how many waves
of hell and death and
dirt and shit
meaningless waves of hurt and punished lives shall America
be nothing but the story of
not at all her successes
—I have been—Leroy has been
as we genetic failures are
successes, here
it isn't interesting,
Yankees—Europeans—Chinese

What is the heart, turning

beating itself out leftward

in hell to know heaven

in this filthy land

in this foul country where

human lives are so much trash

It is the dirty restlessness

of fear and shame—human shame which doesn't even know how right

it is to hate   what ignorance

pervades

the social climbing of this

Ararat this mountain

of rubbish taken from used up anything and made a hill and home for

off the back porch Worcester

rats big scared rats my father and I shot

as the rats came closer

as they filled the Athletic Field

—and Beaver Brook Goddamn US papers

fire
and to lock to
to handle
piece of machinery
was such a delicate
as I'd like to the bolt
my own son
and I don't have now to give
he gave me
with my 22

198

in
in your Praise
Counter
clockwise
Circle

My beloved Father
turning this page to Right
to write this poem

rest   Beloved   Father   as   Your   Son
goes forth to create Paradise

Upon this Earth
Secular Praise
of You and the

Creator
Forever

Heaven
a life America shall yield
and even to
—end even to
And an end to Hell
or we will leave her
and ask Gloucester
to sail away
from this
Rising Shore
Forever Amen

Bottled up for days, mostly
in great sweat of being, seeking
to bind in speed—petere—desire,
to construct knowing back to image and
God's face behind it turned as mine
now is to blackness image shows
herself, desire the light
speed & motion alone are, love's
blackness arrived at going backwards the rate
reason hath—and art her beauty God the Truth

Got me home, the <u>light</u>
snow gives the air, falling

                    how my own hills
          and how Gloucester Harbor suddenly
          coming in on 127 is hewn out
          all perfect in one sight

                    look as though
          and, on the right as you pass Lookout
          or what was Hammond's
          Castle the straight to England

                    which was true, Endicott
          sighted the Winthrop fleet's
          top-mast from Salem as

          they sat here just where 127 shows
          a brand new deck of cards ready
          in your hand put there
          as though Creation itself dropped

                    and,

                    with the cellophane off the
          full American continent going
          North by the Pole and

                    West

                    Charles Olson

written the day I returned from
—Magnolia—and read The Binnacle again as
printed by Robt Creeley in
the Albuquerque Review December 28 1961

                              (February 16
                                 1966

When do poppies bloom   I ask myself, stopping again
to look in Mrs. Frontiero's yard, beside her house on
this side from Birdseyes (or what was once Cunningham
& Thompson's and is now O'Donnell-Usen's) to see if
I have missed them, flaked out and dry-like like
Dennison's Crepe. And what I found was dark buds
like cigars, and standing up   and my question is
when, then, will those blossoms more lotuses to the
West than lotuses wave like paper and petal by petal
seem more powerful than any thing except the Universe
itself, they are so animate-inanimate and dry-beauty not
any shove, or sit there poppies blow as crepe
paper.   And in Mrs Frontiero's yard annually I
expect them as the King of the Earth must have
Penelope, awaiting her return, love lies
so delicately on the pillow as this one flower,
petal and petal, carries nothing
into or out of the World   so threatening
were those cigar-stub cups just now, & I know
how quickly, and paper-like, absorbent
and krinkled paper, the poppy itself will, when here,
go again and the stalks stay like onion plants oh
come, poppy, when will you bloom?

The Fort
June 15th [Wednesday]
XLVI

The hour of evening—supper hour, for my neighbors—quietness
in the street, and kids gone and the night
coming to end the day (which has piled itself up
in shallows, and some
accomplishment—sweet air of evening promises
anew life's endlessness, life itself's
Beauty which all forever so long as there is
a human race like flowers and, I suppose,
other animals—they too must know something
of what it is to love, to be alive, to have
life, to be on the sweetness of Earth herself,
great Goddess we take for granted, God the Father so much
more the strain of our beings, she the sweetness
we arrive in pursuit of
—when in such as this
hour falling suddenly the air suddenly
the voices of each child now
distinct, the
light itself, as the air, suddenly
separating—disassociation of day, wit
approaching—love approaching because
Night accompanies
Heaven coming
to love Earth, the ambush
they the Sons the usurpers
turned on their
Father, in the dark knowing
his habit, to come,

with Night, to make Love to
their Mother—& they harmed him,
Heaven went away that night, Night
stayed, Earth in fact was a Party to her sons'
action—these losses
regained each day when
time brings
the shortness of
Day to an end (Night's daughter
leaves Earth to
Night—and Heaven can,
again, fall in His Desire onto
Earth. Except for this interference
of ourselves, children of this
long & Eternal sequence of
Love & Desire, of our own lives'
scandal in
the Story
as those Sons ruined
their Father and gained Earth or
Their Right, and divided
us—as we too divide the
air of Heaven the mode of
Love-making which
penetrates Earth as
if now it, earth, the
ball also solely it is
as the sun also is, and the moon solely
planets—stars, three in
all the heavens' million millions

which we can see, at night—all nothing
but what is, equally—all physica
if now Earth again has, in her will turned
to shift her axis and,
already in a
10,000 year readjustment of
her magnetic field, we'll—
or so Bruce Heezen speculates that
then (4000 years from now, mid-point, or double
Platonic month—two, as
there's been two since
Indo-European man came
from the Caucasus onto
the Plains—a
like Time—he brought
these versions of the animate
nature of Creation, of
ourselves)—if in 4000 years we'll
lose because the sun's
Gamma—Edda gone to
Gamma—
will pour through the enveloping
Atmosphere—Heaven the Father of Us
not the stars, not the Universe, solely
this extended skin of our own
composite body—miracle of
form will
break—broken into, spoiled in
nature and by Universe, dogged down by
rays—Lord, Father, correct Earth and

Love as

at this hour, each day, in our mercy

of being your Child

in the Paternity of only

Aether, love us and

keep us in Your

Receptacle of

Which You Are The

Source—and Night the

Sweetness of the

Intercourse of which

We Are the Separable,

& tentative Eternal creatures,

Men,

and Women, simulacrum of the

Story, semblable of

You

—of which Life is not

solely Ours not

Everywhere

not all

here on Earth

& in these

troubled

stories

of our Selves, of our

Parents and their repeated

occurrence

Each Turn of Earth

Before Our Own Eyes

Each Day She
Turns Her Back on
Sun, And Night
brings Heaven
to Her to
Begin Again, Love
And Man Shall Continue To Be the Mystica of
This One System Flying
Loose in the melee of the
Universe
And the Perfect Bowl
of the Sky of Gloucester
in which these Events
May be Seen
Each Evening Hour
Each Day before
Night comes
to cover Heaven's
approach, to make Love to
Earth
And bear Us
as our Ancestors were
So Borne

The boats' lights in the dawn now going so swiftly the
night going so swiftly the draggers'
lights shoving so sharply in what's left
clouds even like the puff
of cottons she left which, forgotten,
even with all her care   care of such an order
love itself was put down as over-
ably as, if she chose   and she had
still no choice to organize
every thing: love made as straight
as if   if you could get her womb out
if she cld that is   and it was so close
to the mouth   both my own and her
legs all the distance of her
hair to the tip of the rounded boy
behinds   I could hold both of them in
my one hand   her hair itself
even on her head more clouded
and dense than any depth at all
there was before her womb's mouth
was at the entrance: love's puff
of irritated
wetness   puffs
in the sky and the night
still dark and handsome as the
face of her legs lifted
wetly to be loved and those hurrying
silly two lights boats busily

like little hurrying nifts going too fast
and now too small even though bright
in the still dark but coming now earliest
or latest of earliest light and latest of
night as the darkness and the white puffs
on and by the bed the girl whose head
and whose love she lifts opening
and raising her legs are so
alike night still light already
too far out and the small draggers
too small and bright in the first dawn since
she left was here and
I was
covered as I am not now
alone ill of
separation I cannot
allow love having
not on my own part taken
it
part in her
face & face
hair & hair depth
to my eye and hands
one hand
so much as caught
in her
hair my member my
middle finger right on her crown
love as large and tight as her great
mouth's turning

in perfect tuned love lying
all out three great parts each at
a different rate and
interchange of
time

Out of the light of Heaven   the flower

grows down, the air

of Heaven

Hotel Steinplatz, Berlin, December 25 (1966)

snow
coming
to my window, going up
and as well across
in front of my glasses in front of my eyes and
two thicknesses of glass windows also
between me and
the outside, trying to see actual flakes

But this is the slightest snow, snow starting perhaps, light
(at 2 PM) already
lessening and perhaps—yes, now, speed
begins to—oh no, again they hold,
in the air, and could as well
as some do sidewise—rots at the side the Tree of the World
my injury, in my side, not the lance not the lance by which watery fluid,
I imagined, ran out the hole in his side. As these rain-balls

     which could as well fall back to rain, play,
     in the air, so far only two, have come near enough
     to be, snow even if more as tufts of cloth

         —as the female animal in the boughs
         of the Tree, out of eating the leaves makes milk
         which warriors do not know is

            —oh now the snow speeds
     & thickens!—
            is strong drink they suck

from her hungry tits, sweetened by my devouring
each of them—separately of course but swallowing or enclosing each all
in my mouth (while she watches, above, her eyes on me like

she would not let me see—oh now the snow is all thick
flakes. And light increases, in my room falls thickly erasing
gloom.   But brings terror the sky itself is falling the End

of the World Tree has come! Oh, white hart of the Tree's boughs
oh rotten side of the Tree's side   oh Serpent, of the Earth
do not make this the Epoch simply that man has—oh now the snow

has swung back, no longer falls as though the top has gone, tries
itself once more lessly—It is not good, I want
the snow, I want need, hail and ice, need-nail   fingernail of Abwehr

   the staves
   the three staves of my giants, I need two sweet environments, of precreation,

                                    creation

                                       and

   TiuBirka's bebt, TiuBirka
                   s shaking, of the top and
   dew dew aurr sprinkling until she cries

          who is this man   who drives me   all the way
          who drives me on down this weary path?

          Snowed on by snow, beaten by rain
           drenched with the dew, long I lay dead
   And pressed me, as he went
   not caring, so soon as he had heard
   what he had forced out of me
the Tree itself alone—ah now no snow at all

Celestial evening, October 1967

Advanced out toward the external from
the time I did actually lose space control,
here on the Fort and kept turning left
like my star-nosed mole batted
on the head, not being able to
get home 50 yards as I was
from it. There is a vast

internal life, a sea or organism
full of sounds & memoried
objects swimming or sunk
in the great fall of it as,
when one further
ring of the 9 bounding
Earth & Heaven runs
into the daughter of God's
particular place, cave, palace—a tail

of Ocean whose waters then
are test if even a god
lies will tell & he or she spend
9 following years out of the company
of their own. The sounds

and objects of the great
10th within us are
what we hear see are motived by
dream belief care for discriminate

our loves & choices cares & failures unless
in this forbidding Earth & Heaven by

enclosure 9 times round plus
all that stream collecting as,
into her hands it comes: the

full volume of all which ever was which we
as such have that which is our part of it,
all history existence places splits of moon
& slightest oncoming smallest stars at
sunset, fears & horrors, grandparents'
lives as much as we have also features
and their forms, whatever grace or ugliness our legs
etc possess, it all

comes in as also outward leads
us after itself as though then
the horn of the nearest moon was
truth.   I bend my ear, as,
if I were Amoghasiddi and,
here on this plain where
like my mole I have
been knocked flat, attend,
to turn & turn within
the steady stream & collect which
within me ends as in her hall and I

hear all, the new moon new in all
the ancient sky

The Telesphere

Gather a body to me
like a bear. Take it on
my left leg and hold it off
for love-making, man or woman
boy or girl in the enormity
of the enjoyment that it is
flesh, that it is to be loved, that
I desire it, that without it
my whole body is a hoop
empty and like steel
to be iron to grasp
someone else in myself
like those arms which hold
all the staves together
and make a man, if now as cold and hot
as a bear, out of me.

[Wednesday November
15th (1967)

*

Added to

making a Republic

in gloom on Watchhouse

Point

     an actual earth of value to

     construct one, from rhythm to

     image, and image is knowing, and

     knowing, Confucius says, brings one

     to the goal: nothing is possible without

     doing it.   It is where the test lies, malgre

     all the thought and all the pell-mell of

     proposing it. Or thinking it out or living it

     ahead of time.

               Reading about my world,

               March 6th, 1968

Wholly absorbed
into my own conduits to
an inner nature or subterranean lake
the depths or bounds of which I more and more
explore and know more
of, in that sense that other than that all else
closes out and I tend further to fall into
the Beloved Lake and I am blinder from

spending time as insistently in and on
this personal preserve from which
what I do do emerges more well-known than
other ways and other outside places which
don't give as much and distract me from

keeping my attentions as clear

"Additions", March 1968—2

I live underneath
the light of day

    I am a stone,
or the ground beneath

My life is buried,
with all sorts of passages
both on the sides and on the face turned down
to the earth
or built out as long gifted generous northeastern Connecticut stone walls are
through which 18th century roads still pass
as though they themselves were realms,

the stones they're made up of
are from the bottom such Ice-age megaliths

and the uplands the walls are the boundaries of
are defined with such non-niggardly definition

of the amount of distance between a road in & out
of the wood-lots or further passage-ways, further farms
are given

      that one suddenly is walking

in Tartarian-Eroian, Geaan-Ouranian
time and life love space
    time & exact
analogy   time & intellect   time & mind   time & time
spirit

      the initiation

    of another kind of nation

the Blow is Creation
& the Twist   the Nasturtium
is any one of Ourselves
And the Place of it All?
    Mother   Earth   Alone

INDEX OF FIRST LINES

223

Designer: Barbara Jellow
Compositor: Wilsted & Taylor
Text: Syntax
Display: Syntax
Printer: Thomson-Shore
Binder: Thomson-Shore